BOOKS

THIS IS A CARLTON BOOK

Distributed by National Book Network, Inc.
15200 NBN Way
Blue Ridge Summit, PA 17214
(800) 462-6420

Copyright © Carlton Books Ltd, 2000

First edition 2000

A CIP record for this book is available from the British Library

ISBN 1 84222 297 X

Art Director: Russell Porter
Executive Editor: Chris Hawkes
Editorial Assistant: Luke Friend
Design: Johnny Pau, Nigel Davis
Picture Research: Debora Fioravanti
Production: Sarah Corteel

Printed and bound in the United States of America

Subway
YANKEES vs METS
2000

The dramatic story
of the first Subway World Series since 1956

GEORGE VECSEY

CARLTON
BOOKS

CONTENTS

THERE ARE A FEW BASIC INGREDIENTS FOR THAT BASEBALL TRADITION KNOWN AS A SUBWAY SERIES. FIRST OF ALL, A CITY NEEDS A MASS TRANSPORTATION SYSTEM UNDER ITS TEEMING STREETS. SECOND, THAT CITY NEEDS TWO BASEBALL TEAMS. AND THIRD, THAT CITY NEEDS THE BRASH ASSUMPTION THAT THE WHOLE WORLD IS WAITING FOR ANOTHER SUBWAY SERIES.

CLEARLY, NEW YORK CITY qualifies on all three counts, lacking for neither an underground rail system nor baseball teams nor gall. Yet, mysteriously, New York had gone 44 years without one.

In Greater New York, people tended to call it the Subway Series, although this rankled many of the players and officials who had labored to achieve their goal.

"It's a World Series," said Bobby Valentine, the manager of the Mets, with heavy emphasis on the first word.

"It means that it's the end of October, and the best team in the National League is playing against the best team in the American League," Valentine noted.

Valentine grew up in Connecticut, an hour away from midtown New York, and his Yankee counterpart, Joe Torre, grew up in the borough of Brooklyn, and both understood the importance of the Subway Series.

There is no rivalry greater than a local rivalry. The English and the Italians and other soccer-playing countries understand it with their "derby" - an occasional match between AC Milan and Inter of Italy, or Manchester United and Manchester City of England.

That's when it gets personal. That's when people rub each other the wrong way.

Introduction

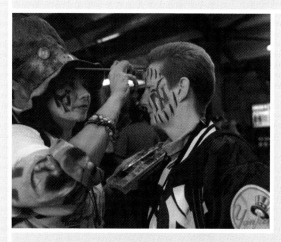

New York has a glorious history of it. For more than half a century, the city had three baseball teams, the Giants of Manhattan, the Yankees eventually of the Bronx and the Dodgers of Brooklyn.

Thirteen times from 1921 through 1956, the Yankees played either the Giants or the Dodgers in the so-called Fall Classic. The Yankees won ten of them, a minor fact which Yankee fans, to this day, will suddenly recall in the middle of a conversation about something else.

(For the record: there were also regional World Series in Chicago in 1906, St. Louis in 1944 and the San Francisco-Oakland Bay Area in 1989, but New Yorkers tend to think these events either did not count or perhaps did not happen at all.)

But, in the 1958 season, the Dodgers moved to Los Angeles and the Giants moved to San Francisco, leaving a huge gap in New York and making a Subway Series impossible. In 1962, the Mets were formed, at first a lowly collection of rejects who managed to develop a huge and enthusiastic following, which irritated haughty Yankee fans no end.

The Mets managed to win World Series in both 1969 and 1986, but the two teams had never met until 2000, when both advanced through the expanded Championship Series of their respective leagues.

Needless to say, the New York region was convinced this was the greatest event ever to occur on the planet. Many people went out and bought new caps, new jerseys, new banners, to proclaim their loyalties to either the pinstriped Yankees or the orange-and-blue Mets.

Armageddon was widely feared, yet what actually took place was a rather lusty but safe celebration of baseball and mutual existence. Perhaps it was because there were large numbers of both sides. Or maybe everybody got the drift that it is, after all, only a game.

The bottom line was that New York had a wonderful time, with Yankee fans having a far better time than Met fans.

Playing in balmy weather, the two teams began their long-awaited Subway Series.

In the first game, at historic Yankee Stadium alongside the Harlem River, the Yankees won in extra innings because their relief pitching was better than the Mets.

The second game was marred by a first-inning incident when the Yankees burly pitcher, Roger Clemens, heaved a chunk of broken bat quite near the Mets power

Introduction

hitter, Mike Piazza. Nobody could prove he meant harm (although he was eventually fined $50,000 for his rash act) and in the meantime Clemens helped the Yanks beat the Mets for a second straight night.

Then the Mets won the third game with an eighth-inning rally at their somewhat more prosaic Shea Stadium on the flight path next to LaGuardia Airport. This victory elevated the hopes of Mets fans, who began recalling the stunning upset in 1969 and the fantastic comeback in 1986.

No way. These Yankees were too poised, too skilled, too experienced. They came back and won the fourth game as Torre cobbled together a fine effort from five pitchers.

In the fifth game, the Yanks won their 26th World Championship, the most of any American sports franchise, as Derek Jeter, their superb young shortstop, was named the Most Valuable Player of the World Series.

The Yankee players did not necessarily need any emotional lift to get them where they were going. They had, after all, steamrollered their way to vital victories on foreign soil in Atlanta in 1996, San Diego in 1998 and Atlanta again in 1999.

However, the players appreciated the huge cadre of Yankee fans in the Mets ball park – perhaps as much as 20 percent. This presence was explained by the Mets management having sold thousands of tickets by phone, and their have been gobbled up by wealthy fans with Wall Street and Internet money (and extra phones and junior staff members to dominate the lines.).

Everybody agreed these tight games formed one of the best five-game World Series in history, but there was not much suspense in the final count: Yankees 4, Mets 1.

It was annoying to Mets fans to leave their home park, hearing the familiar chant of "Let's go, YAN-kees! Let's go, YAN-kees!" But the fans mingled with uplifting teasing rather than ugly spirits.

After the traditional tickertape parade for the Yankees in lower Manhattan on Monday, New York began planning for 2001. New Yorkers tend to think the Subway Series should be an annual event. No surprise there.

GEORGE VECSEY
New York, October 2000

Subway Series History

1921
GIANTS 5 YANKEES 3

1922
GIANTS 4 YANKEES 0

1923
YANKEES 4 GIANTS 2

1936
YANKEES 4 GIANTS 2

1937
YANKEES 4 GIANTS 1

1941
YANKEES 4 DODGERS 1

1947
YANKEES 4 DODGERS 3

1949
YANKEES 4 DODGERS 1

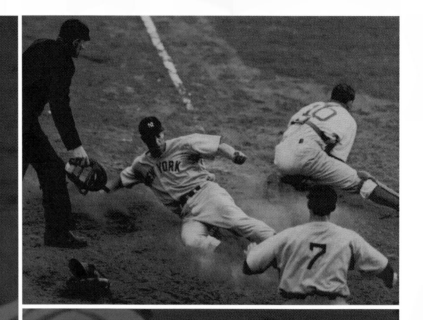

1951

YANKEES 4 GIANTS 2

1952

YANKEES 4 DODGERS 3

1953

YANKEES 4 DODGERS 2

1955

YANKEES 4 DODGERS 3

1956

YANKEES 4 DODGERS 3

THE YANKEES ARE OBVIOUSLY THE ENGINE THAT DRIVES THE SUBWAY SERIES. HARD AS IT IS TO BELIEVE, THOUGH, THEY WENT INTO THEIR FIRST WORLD SERIES AS LOWLY TENANTS TO THE NEW YORK GIANTS.

Subway Series History

THE YANKEES DON LARSEN ETCHED HIS NAME IN WORLD SERIES HISTORY WITH HIS PERFECT GAME AGAINST THE DODGERS IN 1956

It took the Yankees three appearances to get it down pat, but since then, they have run over three separate New York teams in one Subway Series or another.

To talk about the World Series is to talk about the Yankees, whether it was Babe Ruth and Lou Gehrig swatting home runs or Joe DiMaggio providing power and grace or Mickey Mantle slugging a game-winner into the upper deck or Reggie Jackson hitting three in one game or Derek Jeter coming up with the long ball when the Yankees needed it the most.

The Yankees have dominated the baseball championship as no other American team has dominated its sport. With 26 titles in 37 World Series, they have outdone the Montreal Canadiens of hockey, the Boston Celtics of basketball, Notre Dame of college football and any of the temporary dynasties of professional football. Yankees rule.

Yet they were upstarts the first time around, literally the third team in a three-team city. Like many ultimately successful New Yorkers, they arrived from another place, in this case survivors of a failed franchise in Baltimore.

From 1903 through 1912, they were called the Highlanders, making do in a makeshift park in upper Manhattan, but in 1913 they moved to the Polo Grounds and were called the Yankees, second-class citizens, if you can imagine.

The Giants were the darlings of the carriage trade – the power brokers who lived in handsome townhouses and dictated the mid-afternoon starting times, after they had dispensed with business for the day. When the Giants were on the road, the Yankees were permitted to play their home games.

The Giants won pennants in 1905, 1911, 1912, 1913 and 1917, winning only their first World Series, but with no appreciable blow to their landlord hearts.

Even the raffish Brooklyn Trolley Dodgers (or

BABE RUTH (L) AND LOU GEHRIG (R) WERE AN INTEGRAL PART OF THE YANKEES EARLY SUCCESSES, PROVIDING AN INCOMPARABLE 1–2 PUNCH

Bridegrooms or Superbas or whatever they were calling themselves at the moment) won pennants in 1916 and 1920. The Yankees just idled along, paying rent.

But events were happening that would implement the institution known as the Subway Series. In 1919, the Chicago White Sox lost to the Cincinnati Reds in a World Series tainted by a gambling scandal that led to eight members of the so-called Black Sox being banned for life.

As a result, the office of Baseball Commissioner was created, in the person of Judge Kenesaw Mountain Landis. Among his first acts was to install a more lively ball to guarantee more home runs, which had become popular due to a brash young pitcher and part-time slugger named George Herman (Babe) Ruth with the Boston Red Sox.

Another event that would change the game was the sale of Ruth to the Yankees on January 3, 1920, a date that will live in infamy in Boston.

Babe Ruth not only saved baseball with his marvelous athleticism and outsized persona, he also built the legend of the New York Yankees. In 1921, Ruth made possible the very first Subway Series.

THE GIANTS MANAGER JOHN McGRAW LED HIS TEAM TO BACK-TO-BACK SERIES WINS OVER THE YANKEES

1921
This would be the last of a three-year experiment with a best-of-nine Series. Ruth had stunned the sport by hitting 54 home runs in his first season and this year he led the Yankees to their first pennant by hitting 59 more. However, he hit only one homer in six Series games, troubled by an abscess on his left elbow.

This Series was a matchup between two great managers, John McGraw of the Giants and Miller Huggins of the Yankees. The Yanks won the first two games and led, 4–0, in the third before the Giants asserted themselves to win in eight.

1922
Ruth batted only .118 with one home run, as the Yankees lost four of five decisions. There was also a tie of the second game, called by the umpires because of failing light in the October afternoon, in an era before there were lights in any stadium.

Subway Series History

Once again, the Giants were led by their fiery young second baseman, Frankie Frisch, from Fordham University in the Bronx. These two straight victories over the Yankees only served to secure the Giants in their assumption that they were the masters of the universe, or at very least that portion of it connected by the various subway lines.

JOE DiMAGGIO PLAYED IN SIX SUBWAY SERIES WITH THE YANKEES, SPANNING THREE DECADES, FROM 1936 TO 1951

1923 The Yankees needed a change of scenery, and they got it with a move directly across the Harlem River to their own ball park, immediately called Yankee Stadium but forevermore known as "The House That Ruth Built." Never was an edifice constructed with better collateral.

This time the Giants had to trek across the 155th Street Bridge to open the 1923 Series, and they actually won it, holding Ruth to no homers. But the next day they moved back to the Polo Grounds and Ruth celebrated with two home runs. He wound up hitting another as the Yankees won their first World Series in six games.

Of note was the .417 batting average of Casey Stengel, a former Dodger and now an irascible 33-year-old Giant, who had no way of knowing he would one day be an immortal manager of both the Yankees and an unimagined team called the Mets.

1936 By now, all the dynamics had changed. The Yankees were now the terrors of baseball, having demolished Pittsburgh in 1927, St. Louis in 1928 and the Cubs in 1932, all in four games. They had missed three years while phasing out Ruth, but in 1936 they met the Giants again, this time with a centerfielder named Joe DiMaggio, straight from the docks of San Francisco Bay.

The Giants were no slouch, with Bill Terry in his later years, screwball pitcher Carl Hubbell and unorthodox slugger Mel Ott in their primes, but the Yankees prevailed in six games.

1937 The Yankees won in five games behind Tony Lazzeri, the superb second baseman who batted .400 in his last Series, and Lefty Gomez, a wise-cracking pitcher, who tossed two shutouts. The Yanks used one bench player for one at-bat, as Gehrig and DiMaggio prevailed.

Subway Series History

1941 New subway connections were explored as the Dodgers reached the World Series. The Dodgers were led by manager Leo Durocher, a former Yankee teammate of Ruth, while Joe McCarthy was the long-time Yankee manager.

THE YEAR HE BROKE BASEBALL'S COLOR BARRIER, JACKIE ROBINSON MADE IT TO THE WORLD SERIES WITH THE DODGERS, EVENTUALLY LOSING TO THE YANKEES IN SEVEN

This Series would set the heartbreaking tone for the Dodgers in many future Subway Series. The Yankees took a 2–1 lead in the series, but in the fourth game, the Dodgers held a 4–3 lead with two outs in the ninth. Then Hugh Casey threw a third strike to Tommy Henrich that broke so viciously that many people have claimed it was an illegal spitball. The ball whizzed past catcher Mickey Owen, and Henrich reached first. Then DiMaggio singled, Charlie Keller doubled for two runs and Joe Gordon doubled for two more as the Yankees won, 7–4. The Yanks also won the fifth game, setting up a cry that would echo from Brooklyn in many an October: "Wait 'til next year."

1947 The Dodgers had been rebuilt after the war with young players from Branch Rickey's farm system. Rickey had also signed Jack Roosevelt Robinson, the first African-American to play in the modern major leagues.

The Yankees were, as always, the Yankees. They found a way to win, opening with two victories at home. Then the Dodgers won the third game. In the fourth game, Bill Bevens of the Yankees, a journeyman pitcher, had an erratic no-hitter and a 2–1 lead with two outs in the ninth. But Cookie Lavagetto, a veteran pinch-hitter, whacked a double off the right-field wall in Ebbets Field, to break up the no-hitter, drive in two runs and win the game, 3–2.

The Yanks came back to win the fifth game but the Dodgers won the sixth, when Al Gionfriddo, an obscure left fielder, hauled in a home run by DiMaggio, who kicked the dirt in an almost unique show of frustration. Then the Yankees won the seventh game, 2–1, behind Frank Shea, a Connecticut Yankee.

As a footnote, neither Bevens nor

JOLTIN' JOE (R) CELEBRATES WITH FRANK SHEA (L), WHO WON GAME 7 FOR THE YANKEES IN THE 1947 SERIES AGAINST THE DODGERS

Subway Series History

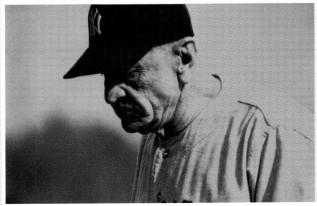

CASEY STENGEL SPENT 54 YEARS IN BASEBALL, MUCH OF IT IN NEW YORK, WHERE HE PLAYED OR MANAGED FOR THE GIANTS, THE DODGERS, THE YANKEES AND THE METS

Lavagetto nor Gionfriddo ever played in another Major League game.

1949 Zero for zero, Don Newcombe matched Allie Reynolds until the bottom of the ninth inning. Tommy Henrich slugged a homer, which demonstrated why Henrich was already called Old Reliable. Preacher Roe won the second game for the Dodgers, but the Yankees cruised to three straight victories behind relief pitcher Joe Page and hitting star Bobby Brown, already in medical school en route to a long career as a cardiologist. The Yankees new manager was none other than Casey Stengel, back from a stint in the Pacific Coast League, but about to become a New York fixture.

1951 Some would say the greatest Subway Series of all took place in the three-game playoff between the Dodgers and Giants, won on Bobby Thomson's home run. While Dodgers fans grieved, the Giants took a 2–1 lead in the World Series, and appeared to have the momentum, but the Yankees bounced back after a rainout, as Allie Reynolds pitched a complete game.

The two other aces, Eddie Lopat and Vic Raschi, then beat the Giants to end the Series in six games. Joe DiMaggio hit a home run in his last Series and Mickey Mantle tore up his knee in his first. The Giants were managed by Durocher, the former Yankee and Dodger. Stengel, another three-team New Yorker, was just settling in.

1952 The Dodgers were better than ever, having garnered great players from the Negro League, including Joe Black, moved from the bullpen to starting pitcher by Charlie Dressen. They took a 3–2 lead going back to Brooklyn, but Stengel matched his old rival by using Allie Reynolds in relief in both games. In the seventh inning of the seventh game, the Dodgers loaded the bases and Robinson's pop-up appeared to be lost in the glare. Then Billy Martin, the scrawny second baseman and a pet of Stengel's from Oakland, came racing in to make a desperation catch that would secure the Series.

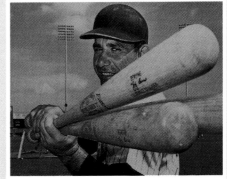

IN THE '56 SERIES, YOGI BERRA PROVIDED THE HOT BAT AND CAUGHT LARSEN'S PERFECT GAME

1953 More of the same. Mantle hit a grand slam as the Yankees won the pivotal fifth game in Brooklyn. In the sixth game, Stengel used Reynolds in relief of young Whitey Ford for the Yankees fifth consecutive World Championship – still a record. Martin was the hitting star, making 12 hits in 24 at-bats and driving in eight runs.

1955 Walter Alston, deceptively quiet, was the Dodgers' manager. The Yankees won the first two at home, but the Dodgers won the next three at tiny Ebbets Field. Ford won the sixth game in the Stadium. In the seventh game, Gil Hodges, who had settled in Brooklyn, drove in runs in the fourth and sixth. In the bottom of the sixth, Alston made a defensive change, putting the fleet Sandy Amoros in left field. With two runners on, Yogi Berra sliced a drive to left field, seemingly good for two runs, but Amoros tracked it down, then threw the ball to Pee Wee Reese, the Dodger captain, who relayed to Hodges for the rally-killing double play. Three innings later, the bells were ringing all over Brooklyn.

THE YANKEES MICKEY MANTLE HIT 18 CAREER WORLD SERIES HOMERS INCLUDING A GRAND SLAM IN '53

1956 Back to basics. The Dodgers won the opener behind Sal (The Barber) Maglie, a former nemesis from the Giants. They won a slugfest in the second game. But the Yankees went home and won three straight, the third being a perfect game by Don Larsen, known for his late nights and his early departure from the second game. To end the game, Larsen slipped a called third strike past Dale Mitchell. It is still the only no-hitter in World Series history.

Clem Labine, normally a relief pitcher, pitched a 1–0 shutout in the sixth game. But in the seventh, Berra clubbed two more homers off Newcombe, who would never win a World Series game.

With their tenth victory in 13 Subway Series, the Yankees were princes of their city. However, in order to hold a Subway Series, the Yankees needed a New York opponent. After the 1957 season, the Dodgers moved to Los Angeles and the Giants to San Francisco.

The Subway Series – that home-town luxury turned into a birthright by most New Yorkers – was shunted to a siding, indefinitely.

The Divisional Series

AMERICAN
LEAGUE

YANKEES

VS

ATHLETICS

BRINGING THE

SUBWAY SERIES

BACK TO LIFE WAS

NEVER GOING TO BE

AN EASY TASK.

IT INVOLVED

FORTY-FOUR YEARS

OF MACHINATIONS

AND MOOD SWINGS

THAT COULD FILL AN

ANTHOLOGY.

NATIONAL
LEAGUE

METS

VS

GIANTS

American League Divisional Series

With a Subway Series very much on its mind, New York looked forward to 2000. The Yankees, getting older, survived a major case of the September staggers to qualify as division champions, while the Mets, a charming work in progress, made it as the wild-card team along with three division champions.

Now both teams had to get through the elaborate post-season maze. Several of the Yankees' key players, like Paul O'Neill, the combustible right fielder, Tino Martinez, the solid first baseman, and David Cone, once their ace pitcher, had sub-par years. Chuck Knoblauch had developed a hitch in his throwing that made him a liability at second base, and Torre had begun to hide him as the designated hitter.

However, George Steinbrenner's money was able to retool the Yankees in mid-season, particularly in a trade for David Justice, an expensive left fielder still close to his prime. And the Yankees still had Derek Jeter at shortstop, Bernie Williams in center field and Mariano Rivera, the ace of the bullpen. And Joe Torre managed with even more patience and wisdom than he had ever needed.

Because of their late slump, the Yankees had lost the privilege of the extra home game, so they opened at Oakland, a team with a much lower payroll but the effervescence of outsiders.

The A's won the first game, 5–3, as Roger

Clemens could not hold an early lead. The burly 38-year-old right-hander had won five Cy Young Awards as the best pitcher in his league, but had a history of poor postseason games.

In 1986, Clemens had left the sixth game of the World Series, and the Red Sox had ultimately kicked the game away. In 1990, he had been ejected from a championship game at Oakland. And although he finally won a World Series game with the Yankees in 1999, he had now put them in a hole in a short best-of-five series.

In the second game, Andy Pettitte, who had nearly been traded by the Yankees a year earlier, shut down Oakland, 4–0.

The teams flew across the country and the Yankees won the third game, 4-2, behind Orlando Hernandez, known as "El Duque" since his childhood in Cuba.

The Yankees desperately wanted to clinch at home on Saturday but Clemens was pounded again and they lost, 11–1. They had come to the ballpark with extra clothes, knowing that if they lost they would have to fly straight back to Oakland. With the weariness of men with too many air miles in their tailbones, they trudged off to catch their charter plane.

A team with less character might have folded somewhere over Kansas, but the Yankees persevered. They arrived in Oakland at 3:30am and after a few hours of sleep went out and scored six runs in the first inning. Pettitte held on long enough for the 7–5 victory that put them into the next round.

"In the five years that I've been here, this is the toughest series we played," Derek Jeter said.

Tuesday, October 3, 2000

GAME 1

ATHLETICS 1   YANKEES 0

YANKEES 3	GAME ONE – THE COLISEUM											ATHLETICS 5
		1	2	3	4	5	6	7	8	9	H	E	
	Yankees	0	2	0	0	0	1	0	0	0	7	0	
	Athletics	0	0	0	0	3	1	0	1	x	10	2	

Scoring Summary: T2nd: Sojo doubled to deep left center, Posada scored. Brosius doubled to shallow left, Sojo scored. B5th: Hernandez singled to shallow right, Chavez scored, Je. Giambi to second. Velarde singled to shallow left, Je. Giambi scored, Hernandez to third. Hernandez scored. T6th: Martinez hit sacrifice fly to left, Williams scored. B6th: Hernandez doubled to right, Chavez scored, Je. Giambi out at home. B8th: Chavez singled to center, Tejada scored.

" Ramon's our secret weapon at the bottom of the order. You need hitting throughout the order to win. We feel good about him being down there, because there's not an easy touch anywhere in the line-up."

A's MANAGER **ART HOWE** ON RAMON HERNANDEZ, WHO WENT 2–4 IN THE GAME AFTER HITTING .241 DURING THE REGULAR SEASON

" We have to come out tomorrow and win."

" I don't know about a big dent, but we certainly wanted to win this game."

A's MANAGER **ART HOWE**

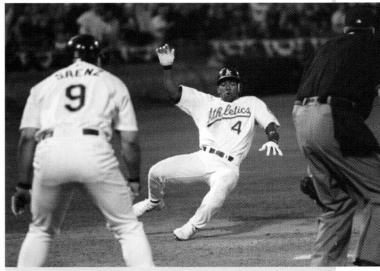

THE A's MIGUEL TEJADA SCORES ON ERIC CHAVEZ'S EIGHTH-INNING SINGLE TO EXTEND OAKLAND'S LEAD

" I think we played a good game."

YANKEES **DEREK JETER**

DEREK JETER REMAINED UPBEAT DESPITE GOING 0–3

" Tired? Yeah, maybe. Struggling? Yeah, maybe. But scared? ... That word ain't even in our vocabulary."

YANKEES OWNER **GEORGE STEINBRENNER**

" There's no doubt about it, we've got to win that game tomorrow."

YANKEES CENTER FIELDER **BERNIE WILLIAMS**

Wednesday, October 4, 2000

GAME 2

ATHLETICS 1   YANKEES 1

YANKEES 4	GAME TWO – THE COLISEUM												ATHLETICS 0
		1	2	3	4	5	6	7	8	9	H	E	
	Yankees	0	0	0	0	0	3	0	0	1	8	1	
	Athletics	0	0	0	0	0	0	0	0	0	6	1	

Scoring Summary: T6th: Hill singled to center, Williams scored, O'Neill to second. Sojo doubled to shallow right, O'Neill and Hill scored. T9th: Bellinger doubled to shallow right, Vizcaino scored.

66 O'Neill's been there so many times in the past and come up with big hits for them. We knew he'd been struggling, but we didn't want to let him beat us. Glenallen did."

A's MANAGER **ART HOWE** ON THE INTENTIONAL WALK TO THE STRUGGLING PAUL O'NEILL. GLENALLEN HILL STEPPED UP TO THE PLATE AND CASHED IN FOR A SINGLE THAT BROUGHT BERNIE WILLIAMS (ABOVE) HOME FOR THE FIRST RUN OF THE NIGHT

"He's tough, he's tough, he doesn't get a lot of attention because you have high-profile people on the club, but he can pitch a big game and I don't think he's pitched one bigger than tonight."

YANKEES MANAGER **JOE TORRE** ON PITCHER ANDY PETTITTE (ABOVE)

"We've been down. We've been on a terrible skid. I hope this will get us going. This is a big game for us, obviously. We've really been struggling."

YANKEES PITCHER **ANDY PETTITTE**, WHO ALLOWED JUST FIVE HITS IN 7⅔ SCORELESS INNINGS

Friday, October 6, 2000

GAME 3

ATHLETICS 1   YANKEES 2

ATHLETICS 2	GAME THREE – YANKEE STADIUM											YANKEES 4
		1	2	3	4	5	6	7	8	9	H	E	
	Athletics	0	1	0	0	1	0	0	0	0	4	2	
	Yankees	0	2	0	1	0	0	0	1	x	6	1	

Scoring Summary: T2nd: Je. Giambi singled to right, Tejada scored. B2nd: Hill reached on fielder's choice to pitcher, Williams scored, O'Neill to second. Jeter reached on an in-field single, O'Neill scored, Hill to third, Brosius to second. B4th: Jeter grounded into fielder's choice to shortstop, Sojo scored, Brosius out at second. T5th: Long homered to right. B8th: Sojo singled to center, Martinez scored.

" We've been a lot crisper ballclub since the postseason started. Hopefully we are on our way to doing something special this year."

YANKEES MANAGER **JOE TORRE** AFTER MANY PUNDITS HAD WRITTEN HIS TEAM OFF FOLLOWING SEVEN STRAIGHT LOSSES HEADING INTO THE POSTSEASON

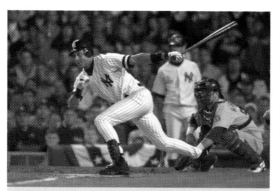

DEREK JETER'S BASE HIT DROVE IN PAUL O'NEILL, EXTENDING THE YANKEES LEAD

"The biggest part is the mental mistakes. That's how you learn. This is our first play-off. Maybe we tried to do too much."

A's CATCHER **RAMON HERNANDEZ**, WHO WENT FOR THE TOUGH PLAY AT SECOND IN THE FOURTH INNING, BUT HIS HIGH THROW HIT TEJEDA'S GLOVE SENDING, SOJO TO THIRD ON THE ERROR

"We just didn't execute tonight. It was as simple as that. We just didn't make the plays we can make."

A's MANAGER **ART HOWE**

"For the first five innings my control was terrible and my team was encouraging me. After the fifth inning, Mr Torre pulled me aside and said stop battling yourself and pitch the game."

YANKEES **ORLANDO HERNANDEZ** (RIGHT), THOUGH A TRANSLATOR, ON BATTLING THROUGH SEVEN TOUGH INNINGS

" I thought he straightened himself out in the sixth inning. He felt so badly about how he pitched in the first five. I sensed he was very frustrated. But he perked up after the sixth inning."

YANKEES MANAGER **JOE TORRE**

Saturday, October 7, 2000

GAME 4

ATHLETICS 2   YANKEES 2

ATHLETICS 11	GAME FOUR – YANKEE STADIUM												YANKEES 1
		1	2	3	4	5	6	7	8	9	H	E	
	Athletics	3	0	0	0	0	3	0	1	4	11	0	
	Yankees	0	0	0	0	0	1	0	0	0	8	0	

Scoring Summary: T1st: Saenz homered to left, Velarde and Ja. Giambi scored. T6th: Grieve singled to shallow right, Chavez and Tejada scored. Hernandez grounded into fielder's choice to shortstop, Grieve scored.
B6th: Posada doubled to left, O'Neill scored. T8th: Christenson singled to right, Tejada scored.
T9th: Chavez doubled to right, Velarde and Ja. Giambi scored, Piatt to third. Tejada grounded out to second, Piatt scored, Chavez to third. Porter reached on an infield single, Chavez scored.

One for my scrapbook, I guess. I tried not to feel the pressure ... I tried to approach it like it was a regular-season game. Trust my body, trust my stuff."

A's PITCHER **BARRY ZITO** (LEFT) WHO AT 22 IS THE YOUNGEST PITCHER IN THE SERIES AFTER SHUTTING DOWN THE YANKEES OFFENSE FOR 5⅔ INNINGS

THE A's OLMEDO SAENZ CIRCLES THE BASES AFTER HIS THREE-RUN HOMER BROKE OPEN GAME 4

66 Hopefully we can get some hits. That's been the most frustrating part of it for me, my players and my coaches. We're going to get hits sooner or later, mark my words."

YANKEES MANAGER **JOE TORRE**

66 We're getting on this plane tonight and we're going out there for a reason. I don't sense anything needs to be said."

YANKEES MANAGER **JOE TORRE**

SAENZ'S HOME RUN GETS THE THUMBS-UP FROM THE A'S JASON GIAMBI

66 We're having a great time, so we'll see what happens. We got good momentum going in the first inning."

A's **OLMEDO SAENZ** WHO ROCKETED A THREE-RUN HOMER OFF CLEMENS IN THE FIRST INNING

66 Nothing has really come easy this year at all. It's disappointing, no question about it."

YANKEES PITCHER **ROGER CLEMENS** (LEFT) WHO WAS POUNDED BY A'S BATTERS

Sunday, October 8, 2000

GAME 5

ATHLETICS 2   YANKEES 3

ATHLETICS 2   YANKEES 3

YANKEES
7

GAME FIVE – THE COLISEUM	1	2	3	4	5	6	7	8	9	H	E
Yankees	6	0	0	1	0	0	0	0	0	12	0
Athletics	0	2	1	2	0	0	0	0	0	13	0

ATHLETICS
5

Scoring Summary: T1st: Williams hit sacrifice fly to right, Knoblauch scored. Martinez doubled to deep center, Jeter, O'Neill and Justice scored. Sojo hit sacrifice fly to center, Martinez scored. Knoblauch singled to right, Posada scored. B2nd: Velarde singled to shallow left, Piatt and Hernandez scored. B3rd: Chavez doubled to deep left center, Tejada scored. T4th: Justice homered to right. B4th: Ja. Giambi hit sacrifice fly to center, Hernandez scored, Long to third. Saenz hit sacrifice fly to left, Long scored.

 A lot of people were trying to say that our run was over, but you're not going to beat us that easily. We're still the champs until someone beats us."

YANKEES **DEREK JETER** (LEFT) WHO SCORED ON TINO MARTINEZ'S DOUBLE. (RIGHT) SCOTT BROSIUS WHO WENT 2-4

30

TINO MARTINEZ'S DOUBLE (LEFT) TO DEEP CENTER FIELD SCORED THREE RUNS, INCLUDING PAUL O'NEILL (ABOVE) AND DAVID JUSTICE (RIGHT) TO PUT THE YANKEES UP 4–0

" It's all about pride and will. We've got something good going, and we don't want to give it away."

YANKEES **PAUL O'NEILL**

" We let them get a running start on us tonight, that's the difference in the ballgame. We battled back, got within two."

A's MANAGER **ART HOWE**

National League Divisional Series

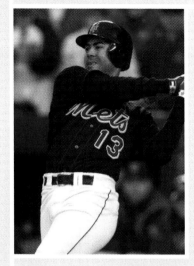

In 1962 the National League connived to produce a dreadful team in New York, to be managed by none other than Casey Stengel, who had won ten pennants with the Yankees before being dismissed in 1960. The Old Man labeled his team "The Amazing Mets," which covered a multitude of sins, including a record 120 losses in their first season.

Given the Mets' ineptitude, it seemed futile to dream of a Subway Series ever again, but in 1969 baseball expanded again, and the Mets, with Stengel cheering from the stands, won the brand-new league championship series and then shocked Baltimore in the World Series.

After that, for decades, whenever the Yankees were up, the Mets were down, and vice versa. But in 1999, both the Yanks and Mets were stocked with talent because of an abundance of New York cable television revenue, and people dared speak the name of a Subway Series.

The Mets began their postseason trail at the other end of the BART line, the rail system that connects the Bay Area. They were matched against the San Francisco Giants, winners of the west. The Mets had improved themselves by acquiring Mike Hampton, a left-hander who was

eligible to be a free agent after 2000. They also had powerful Mike Piazza and steady Edgardo Alfonzo, and manager Bobby Valentine seemed more secure than he had ever been.

The Mets lost the first game, 5-1, in handsome new Pacific Bell Park alongside the

National League Divisional Series

water in downtown San Francisco. Barry Bonds, the Giants' great left fielder with his history of post-season failure, hit a triple to put the Giants ahead.

But the Mets showed their determination by coming back and winning the second game, 5-4, in ten innings. John Franco, once the Mets' star relief pitcher but now a setup man for strapping Armando Benitez, was called on to get the final out against the left-handed Bonds, and Franco saved the game with a called third strike. The Mets flew cross country to New York in decent shape.

On Saturday, the two teams hooked up for a 13-inning marathon, until Benny Agbayani hit a home run. Agbayani, who had started the season knowing the Mets might try to send him down because their roster was crammed with outfielders, was now a highly popular regular in left field.

Not wanting to match the Yankees and fly across country again, the Mets beat the Giants, 4–0, on Sunday to win the Division Series. Bobby J. Jones, a veteran right-hander who had been sent to the minors during a mid-season slump, pitched a masterful one-hitter. Bonds wound up hitting .176 for the Giants, in another postseason disappointment.

The Mets' victory, coupled with the Yankees' a few hours later, meant that New York could now raise the anticipation for a Subway Series.

Wednesday, October 4, 2000

GAME 1

GIANTS 1   METS 0

METS 1	GAME ONE – PACIFIC BELL PARK												GIANTS 5
		1	2	3	4	5	6	7	8	9	H	E	
	Mets	0	0	1	0	0	0	0	0	0	5	0	
	Giants	1	0	4	0	0	0	0	0	x	10	0	

Scoring Summary: B1st: Kent grounded out to shortstop, Mueller scored. T3rd: Payton hit sacrifice fly to right center, Bordick scored. B3rd: Bonds tripled to right, Mueller scored. Burks homered to left, Bonds and Kent scored.

66 Barry has stepped it up for us a lot of days. Today he was very focused, very determined, very poised. He came through for us early and that was big ... I'm not surprised by Ellis' big hit. He's made his at-bats count all year long ... Ellis may not be our Most Valuable Player, but he is definitely our Most Valuable Person."

GIANTS MANAGER **DUSTY BAKER** ON GAME 1 HEROES BARRY BONDS AND ELLIS BURKS

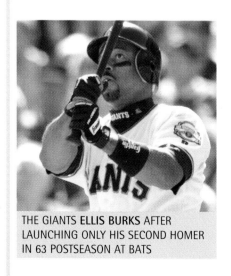

THE GIANTS **ELLIS BURKS** AFTER LAUNCHING ONLY HIS SECOND HOMER IN 63 POSTSEASON AT BATS

66 I felt a little like Carlton Fisk, just without the body language. It was a question of fair or foul, because I knew that ball had the distance. It was a big hit. I've had some big ones here and there, but it's surely one of the top ones in my career."

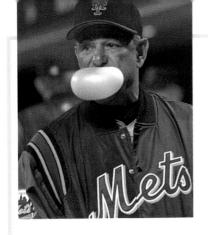

" You could tell by the body language the infielders thought it was a strike. It was a close pitch. That's baseball."

METS MANAGER **BOBBY VALENTINE** (LEFT) ON THE CRUCIAL CALL ON A 2–2 PITCH AGAINST BARRY BONDS, WHO THEN TRIPLED TO GIVE THE GIANTS A 4–1 LEAD

" In every game there is a close call or play that affects the game. Barry has a great eye at the plate. I also saw Hampton's body language and know he wanted that pitch. Pitchers want most pitches, don't they? One ball, one play, but it wasn't the whole ballgame."

GIANTS MANAGER **DUSTY BAKER** DOWNPLAYS THE CALL THAT GAVE BARRY BONDS (BELOW) ANOTHER SHOT AT THE PLATE

" Does he deserve that pitch based on what he's done in the past? Sure. But it's the playoffs and we're trying to win out there. So we don't want anyone given things."

METS **DARRYL HAMILTON** ON THE BONDS AT BAT

Thursday, October 5, 2000

GAME 2

GAME TWO – PACIFIC BELL PARK													
	1	2	3	4	5	6	7	8	9	10	H	E
Mets	0	2	0	0	0	0	0	0	2	1	10	0
Giants	0	1	0	0	0	0	0	0	3	0	8	0

METS 5

GIANTS 4

Scoring Summary: T2nd: Perez singled to center, Payton and Bordick scored. B2nd: Burks doubled to shallow left, Kent scored. T9th: Alfonzo homered to left center, Perez scored. B9th: Snow homered to right, Bonds and Kent scored. T10th: Payton singled to center, Hamilton scored.

" I've been making a living for 17 years getting people out on my changeup. What better time to throw it than that time."

METS **JOHN FRANCO** WHO STRUCK OUT GIANTS SUPERSTAR BONDS IN THE BOTTOM OF THE TENTH TO TIE THE SERIES FOR THE NEW YORKERS

" This is probably the biggest moment of my career. It's the biggest save of my career."

METS VETERAN PITCHER **JOHN FRANCO**, (LEFT) WHO, AT 40, IS THE OLDEST MET

> "When I hit it, I just hoped it stayed fair. Of course, none of that matters right now."

GIANTS **J.T. SNOW** (RIGHT) ON HIS THREE-RUN HOMER THAT TIED THE BALLGAME IN THE NINTH INNING

> "Stuff like this seems to happen to the Mets. Last year you always wondered what crazy thing was going to happen next. It's hard on the fans and it's hard on us ... it's great when we win."

METS **DARRYL HAMILTON** (BELOW) WHO SCORED THE GO-AHEAD RUN

Saturday, October 7, 2000

GAME 3

GIANTS 1   METS 2

	GAME THREE – WILLIAM A. SHEA STADIUM																
	1	2	3	4	5	6	7	8	9	10	11	12	13	H	E
Giants	0	0	0	2	0	0	0	0	0	0	0	0	0	11	0
Mets	0	0	0	0	0	1	0	1	0	0	0	0	1	9	0

GIANTS 2

METS 3

Scoring Summary: T4th: Estalella singled to shallow left, Burks scored, Snow to second. Benard singled to right, Estalella scored. B6th: Perez singled to shallow left, Bordick scored. B8th: Alfonzo doubled to left, Harris scored. B13th: Agbayani homered to left center.

" Fonzie's entire career, it seems like he does the big thing that gets us to the point where we have a chance to win, and then someone else does something right at the end. It seems more spectacular, but it doesn't have any more importance than what Fonzie does."

METS MANAGER **BOBBY VALENTINE** SINGS THE PRAISES OF EDGARDO ALFONZO (ABOVE), WHO DOUBLED IN A RUN OFF GIANTS CLOSER ROBB NEN TO TIE THE GAME AT 2–2

" These are always nerve-wracking. A lot of guys really couldn't swallow out there tonight."

METS CATCHER **MIKE PIAZZA** (RIGHT) ON THOSE EXTRA INNINGS

" You throw all the money out the window because it means nothing. This is why we start playing when we're kids, to get to this point, to have a chance to win the World Series. It's so awesome that every pitch means something. Every pitch counts."

METS UTILITY MAN **JOE McEWING**

" Bobby Valentine told me things have a way of working out. I didn't understand that. Now I do."

13TH-INNING HOME RUN HERO **BENNY AGBAYANI**

"To hit a game-winning home run, I know he's feeling real good right now. I told him, 'Great job, enjoy it man. We've still got one more to go.'"

METS **JAY PAYTON** ON THE GAME-WINNING HOMER BY BENNY AGBAYANI

" It's a great feeling to be the man. We're one of those teams that never say die. We know anything can happen."

METS **BENNY AGBAYANI** WHOSE 13TH-INNING HOMER GAVE THE METS THE SERIES LEAD

Sunday, October 8, 2000

GAME 4

GIANTS 1   METS 3

GIANTS	GAME FOUR – WILLIAM A. SHEA STADIUM											METS
0		1	2	3	4	5	6	7	8	9	H	E	4
	Giants	0	0	0	0	0	0	0	0	0	1	1	
	Mets	2	0	0	0	2	0	0	0	x	6	0	

Scoring Summary: B1st: Ventura homered to right center, Piazza scored. B5th: Alfonzo doubled to center, Jones and Perez scored.

> " If he needed vindication, I'm glad he got it. People like to look at the speed gun and say he's not an upper-echelon pitcher. But it's what he does with that 84mph fastball that torments people."

METS MANAGER **BOBBY VALENTINE** ON FOURTH-GAME HERO BOBBY J. JONES

(LEFT) ALFONZO'S DOUBLE IN THE FIFTH SCORES BOBBY J. JONES AND TINO PEREZ (RIGHT), PUTTING THE METS UP 4-0

" I didn't know what to do. I'd never been in a situation like that before. It's just an overwhelming feeling."

METS PITCHER **BOBBY J. JONES** ON PITCHING THE BEST GAME OF HIS LIFE

" After experiencing the playoffs last year and not being part of it, I wanted to come back in the best shape and have a great year. The way I pitched was obviously not the way I was capable of throwing."

METS PITCHER **BOBBY J. JONES** PITCHED THE FIRST ONE-HIT SHUTOUT IN THE POSTSEASON SINCE ATLANTA'S KEVIN MILLWOOD SHUT DOWN HOUSTON IN GAME 2 OF THE DIVISION SERIES PLAYOFF LAST YEAR

" We were worried about him, no question about it. When we asked him to go to the minor leagues, we never get out timetables on guys, but we knew he was going to have to turn it around or we were going to have to make a decision."

METS GENERAL MANAGER **STEVE PHILLIPS** ON THE DECISION TO SEND PITCHER BOBBY J. JONES TO THE MINOR LEAGUES IN JUNE

"It's not going to be easy. They're a great team and play great baseball. We just have to go out and play the best we can."

METS PITCHER **BOBBY J. JONES** ON THE PROSPECT OF FACING THE ST. LOUIS CARDINALS IN THE CHAMPIONSHIP SERIES

The Champion Series

AMERICAN
LEAGUE

YANKEES

VS

MARINERS

ship

NATIONAL LEAGUE

METS

VS

CARDINALS

THIS OBSESSION WITH A SUBWAY SERIES HAD A LEGITIMATE SOURCE. TO ATTEND A BALLGAME IN NEW YORK IS TO HEAR THE RATTLE AND SCREECH OF THE TRAINS.

American League Championship Series

For their opponent, the Yankees had drawn the Seattle Mariners, who had stunned the Chicago White Sox in three straight games. Although they had lost Ken Griffey, Jr., who chose to play in his home town of Cincinnati, the Mariners had a surprisingly good season, their first full year in the new Safeco Field.

The Mariners still had Alex Rodriguez, the suave and powerful young shortstop, who was in the final year of his contract and would become a free agent. Everybody knew that Rodriguez was a close friend of the Yankees' star, Derek Jeter. When the two teams had contentious moments in the past featuring beanballs and bench-clearing confrontations, Jeter and Rodriguez tended to keep each other out of mischief.

Seattle won the first game in Yankee Stadium, 2–0, behind Freddy Garcia as Rodriguez hit a homer off the foul pole and Rickey Henderson, the great leadoff hitter who once had alternately hustled and dawdled in an earlier stint with the Yankees, drove in the first run.

The Yankees had not scored in 20 innings and were trailing, 1-0, in the eighth inning of Game 2. But the serene Bernie Williams, who had not lost his temper when he hit into a freak double play earlier, tied the game with a single. The Yankees erupted for seven runs and a 7-1 victory, behind their most dependable pitcher in the postseason, Orlando "El Duque" Hernandez.

Then the series moved out to Seattle, where the Yankees won, 8–2, after Williams and Tino Martinez, a former Mariner, hit back-to-back homers in the second inning.

The fourth game had the fireworks. Roger Clemens had not pitched in six days, and his thick frame was bristling with excess energy. He started off with two strikeouts, as his ball veered ominously. Then he fired a pitch under the chin of Rodriguez, who spun out of the way. It was classic Clemens, intimidation with a fastball at nearly 100 miles per hour.

Clemens was totally in control with almost every pitch. He gave up just one hit and finished up with 15 strikeouts.

There were no major recriminations the next day because too much was at stake. Rodriguez bounced back with a two-run single as the Mariners exploded for a 6–2 victory to send the series back to New York with the Yankees ahead, 3–2.

The sixth game back in Yankee Stadium saw the Mariners take an early 4–0 lead, only to have the Yankees come back to 4–3. In a shocking seventh inning, the Yankees scored six runs, three of them on a homer by David Justice, their expensive mid-season import.

A weary Rivera saved the victory for "El Duque," who won his eighth straight postseason decision. The Yankees now had their 37th pennant since Babe Ruth showed them how to do it in 1921.

Now the No. 4 train was revved up to connect with the No. 7 train. There would be a Subway Series.

Tuesday, October 10, 2000

GAME 1

MARINERS 1   YANKEES 0

MARINERS 2	GAME ONE – YANKEE STADIUM											YANKEES 0
		1	2	3	4	5	6	7	8	9	H	E
	Mariners	0	0	0	0	1	1	0	0	0	5	0
	Yankees	0	0	0	0	0	0	0	0	0	6	1

Scoring Summary: T5th: Henderson singled to right, McLemore scored. T6th: Rodriguez homered to left.

" They are going to come out fighting. We have to attack him, attack him early and be ready to go to war, because they are going to come out real hungry."

MARINERS **ALEX RODRIGUEZ** (ABOVE) PREDICTS A TOUGH TIME IN GAME 2 WITH ORLANDO HERNANDEZ STARTING FOR THE YANKEES. RODRIGUEZ'S HOMER CLINCHED GAME 1

" If they pitch like they pitched tonight, then we're not going to win the series."

YANKEES RELIEVER **JEFF NELSON**

" He certainly pitched well when he had to. He pitched pretty well when he didn't have to."

YANKEES MANAGER **JOE TORRE** ON MARINERS PITCHER FREDDY GARCIA (LEFT) WHO STRUCK OUT EIGHT YANKEES IN A DOMINANT 6⅔ INNINGS

" To have a young pitcher come into a play-off game for us like Garcia did, he should be very proud of the his effort tonight."

MARINERS MANAGER **LOU PINIELLA**

" I was feeling pretty good and I had a lot of confidence."

MARINERS STARTING PITCHER **FREDDY GARCIA**

GAME 2

MARINERS 1   YANKEES 1

MARINERS
1

GAME TWO – YANKEE STADIUM

	1	2	3	4	5	6	7	8	9	H	E
Mariners	0	0	1	0	0	0	0	0	0	7	2
Yankees	0	0	0	0	0	0	0	7	x	14	0

YANKEES
7

Scoring Summary: T3rd: Javier singled to center, Cameron scored. B8th: Williams singled to right center, Justice scored. Posada singled to shallow right, Williams scored, T. Martinez to third. O'Neill hit sacrifice fly to left, T. Martinez scored. Vizcaino doubled to deep left center, Sojo scored. Knoblauch singled to center, Vizcaino scored. Jeter homered to right, Knoblauch scored.

DEREK JETER CONGRATULATES DAVID JUSTICE, WHO SCORED ON THE BERNIE WILLIAMS' SINGLE THAT STARTED THE YANKEES EIGHTH-INNING FLOURISH

We know we're better. I think that's what frustrates everybody."

YANKEES MANAGER **JOE TORRE** ON HIS TEAM'S CONFIDENCE

" It was just a great relief for us to score the runs. I just sense we relieved a lot of pressure today."

YANKEES MANAGER **JOE TORRE** ON THEIR SEVEN-RUN EIGHTH INNING THAT INCLUDED A TWO-RUN HOMER BY SHORT STOP DEREK JETER (ABOVE) AND AN RBI SINGLE BY BERNIE WILLIAMS (LEFT)

"We accomplished what we wanted here, we split with them in New York and now we go to our home ballpark. It's a shame because we had seven good innings of base-ball, and in the eighth they exploded on us."

MARINERS MANAGER **LOU PINIELLA**

"Guys were jumping and spinning around. We don't normally react like that. A lot of it was the tension of the situation and the thought of going on the road 0–2."

YANKEES MANAGER **JOE TORRE** ON THE EXCITEMENT ON
THE YANKEE BENCH DURING THEIR EIGHTH-INNING BLITZ

"Down 2–0 in the series would have been devastating. And right now we're riding high with the eighth inning."

DH **CHUCK KNOBLAUCH** (ABOVE) ON
WHAT WINNING MEANS TO THE YANKEES

Friday, October 13, 2000

GAME 3

MARINERS 1   YANKEES 2

YANKEES
8

MARINERS
2

GAME THREE – SAFECO FIELD											
	1	2	3	4	5	6	7	8	9	H	E
Yankees	0	2	1	0	0	1	0	0	4	13	0
Mariners	1	0	0	0	1	0	0	0	0	10	1

Scoring Summary: B1st: E. Martinez singled to shallow left, Cameron scored, Rodriguez to second. T2nd: Williams homered to right. T. Martinez homered to center. T3rd: Justice doubled to left center, Jeter scored. B5th: Cameron singled to shallow left center, Henderson scored. T6th: O'Neill singled to shallow right, Williams scored, T. Martinez to second. T9th: Knoblauch singled to center, Vizcaino scored, Brosius to second. Justice singled to shallow right, Brosius and Knoblauch scored, Jeter to third. Williams hit sacrifice fly, Jeter scored, Bellinger to second advancing on throw.

66 He walks that high wire without a safety net and gets himself in trouble ... when he needed to get out of a jam, he made some quality pitches."

YANKEES MANAGER **JOE TORRE** ON THE PITCHING OF ANDY PETTITTE (LEFT)

66 It's never easy for me, always a battle. After I gave up the run in the first, the guys came right back and battled."

YANKEES PITCHER **ANDY PETTITTE**

TINO MARTINEZ'S SOLO HOMER IN THE SECOND GAVE THE YANKEES THE LEAD – FOR GOOD

66 I hope they always feel like that."

66 It did help. It helped boost our confidence. We were grinding it from the first inning on. We were able to score a lot of runs, it was just a great game for us."

YANKEES **BERNIE WILLIAMS** ON THE CONFIDENCE BOOST GAINED FROM GAME 2

66 Tonight was more like when we are winning."

YANKEES MANAGER **JOE TORRE**

66 You get spoiled with him. The guy just comes in and just doesn't give up runs."

YANKEES PITCHER **ANDY PETTITTE** ON HIS TEAMMATE MARIANO RIVERA

Saturday, October 14, 2000

GAME 4

MARINERS 1   YANKEES 3

YANKEES 5	GAME FOUR – SAFECO FIELD												MARINERS 0
		1	2	3	4	5	6	7	8	9	H	E	
	Yankees	0	0	0	0	3	0	0	2	0	5	0	
	Mariners	0	0	0	0	0	0	0	0	0	1	0	

Scoring Summary: T5th: Jeter homered to center, Brosius and Knoblauch scored. T8th: Justice homered to center, Jeter scored.

 It's puzzling how that can happen when a guy has such good control. He never misses up and away. He always misses up and in. It's some stuff I'm angry about, but I'll get over it."

MARINERS **ALEX RODRIGUEZ** (LEFT) DUSTED BY TWO CLEMENS FASTBALLS IN THE FIRST INNING. (RIGHT) THE YANKEES DEREK JETER BREAKS IT OPEN IN THE FIFTH, WITH A THREE-RUN SHOT

" I wasn't really focused on that, I was focused on winning the game."

YANKEES PITCHER **ROGER CLEMENS** (LEFT) WHEN ASKED WHETHER HE WAS AWARE THAT HE HAD A NO-HITTER GOING

" That was special, Roger. That was absolutely dominant."

YANKEES MANAGER **JOE TORRE** TO GAME 4 HERO ROGER CLEMENS AFTER THE BALLGAME

" The way he threw today, he erased a lot of the questions about him in postseason. A lot of people doubted him, but we didn't."

YANKEES CATCHER **JORGE POSADA** ON TEAMMATE ROGER CLEMENS

ROGER CLEMENS GETS A CELEBRATORY HUG FROM "EL DUQUE" AFTER HIS 15-STRIKEOUT GAME 4 WIN

" I feel fortunate that I've been able to continue at this stage of my career. To go out there and be a part of a great deal of excitement and have a chance to light it up. Sometimes you get beat, but tonight was special."

YANKEES **ROGER CLEMENS**

GAME 5

MARINERS 2   YANKEES 3

<table>
<tr><td rowspan="2">**YANKEES**
2</td><td colspan="12">GAME FIVE – SAFECO FIELD</td><td rowspan="2">**MARINERS**
6</td></tr>
</table>

	1	2	3	4	5	6	7	8	9	H	E
Yankees	0	0	0	2	0	0	0	0	0	8	0
Mariners	1	0	0	0	5	0	0	0	x	8	0

Scoring Summary: B1st: Olerud hit sacrifice fly to right, Cameron scored. T4th: Sojo doubled to left center, T. Martinez and Posada scored, O'Neill to third. B5th: Rodriguez singled to left, McLemore and Henderson scored. E. Martinez homered to center, Rodriguez scored. Olerud homered to right.

“We had plenty of opportunities. We just didn't do anything with them.”

YANKEES MANAGER
JOE TORRE (LEFT)

SEATTLE'S EDGAR MARTINEZ IS CONGRATULATED BY A-ROD AFTER HIS FIFTH-INNING HOME RUN

" You don't want any team celebrating on your field if it is going to be your last game. I think last night it hit me. I had a hard time sleeping a little bit, because ... you might be facing the end, and you don't know what the future holds for me."

MARINERS **ALEX RODRIGUEZ** WHO IS ELIGIBLE FOR FREE AGENCY AFTER THE WORLD SERIES

" The pressure's on them to win. They're supposed to win."

MARINERS MANAGER **LOU PINIELLA**

YANKEE THIRD BASEMAN SCOTT BROSUIS JUST MISSES ALEX RODRIGUEZ'S TWO-RUN SINGLE

Tuesday, October 17, 2000

GAME 6

MARINERS 2   YANKEES 4

MARINERS
7

GAME SIX – YANKEE STADIUM											
	1	2	3	4	5	6	7	8	9	H	E
Mariners	2	0	0	2	0	0	0	3	0	10	0
Yankees	0	0	0	3	0	0	6	0	x	11	0

YANKEES
9

*Scoring Summary: T1st: Rodriguez doubled to left, Martin scored. Martinez doubled to left, Rodriguez scored.
T4th: Guillen homered to right, Olerud scored. B4th: Posada doubled to right center, Justice and Williams scored, Martinez to third. O'Neill singled to center, Martinez scored, Posada to third. B7th: Justice homered to right, Vizcaino and Jeter scored. O'Neill singled to shallow right, Williams and Martinez scored, Posada to second. Vizcaino hit sacrifice fly to left, Posada scored. T8th: Rodriguez homered to left. McLemore doubled to shallow right, Martinez and Olerud scored.*

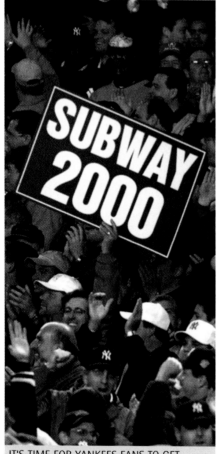

IT'S TIME FOR YANKEES FANS TO GET
READY FOR A SUBWAY SERIES

66 I was at the last one, when Don Larsen pitched the perfect game against Brooklyn ... New York can't lose. Everything is going on between the city limits."

YANKEES MANAGER **JOE TORRE**

66 We were written off. We stuck together."

YANKEES **DAVID JUSTICE** WHOSE SEVENTH-INNING DINGER EFFECTIVELY SEALED THE FIRST SUBWAY SERIES FOR 44 YEARS

66 It's going to be exciting. It's been a long time coming."

YANKEES MANAGER **JOE TORRE**

"It was magical. It was unbelievable when I rounded the bases, to see this place erupt."

YANKEES **DAVID JUSTICE**

National League Championship Series

A few Mets and the occasional visiting player have been known to take the No. 7 elevated line from midtown Manhattan into Queens because it beats driving in rush-hour traffic. And while the Yankees did not have any confirmed subway riders, the No. 4 elevated line and the D subway train both had stations behind deepest center field.

The No. 4 and No. 7 trains connected far below Grand Central Station on the East Side of Manhattan. The Subway Series was on everybody's mind.

But first, the Mets and Yankees had to get there. The Mets were playing the

St. Louis Cardinals, who had been their chief rival during glory days for both of them in the 1980s, but the Cardinals had since moved to the Central Division and the immediacy had cooled a bit.

The Cardinals had just eliminated the Mets' principal tormentors, the Atlanta Braves, in the Division Series, but their great slugger, Mark McGwire, was limited to pinch-hitting roles because of a knee injury. He was replaced by Will Clark, a fiery veteran and a good hitter.

The Championship Series began in St. Louis. The Mets won Game 1, 6–2, behind ace Mike Hampton, and then silenced the red-clad Cardinal fans in Game 2 with a 6–5 victory as rookie Rick Ankiel was extravagantly wild early and Jack Clark made a ninth-inning error before Jay Payton drove in the winning run.

National League Championship Series

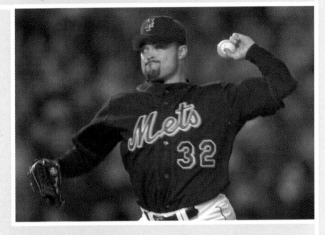

Then the series moved to New York for three games. The Cardinals won, 8–2, behind Andy Benes, but the Mets took the next, 10–6, hitting five doubles in the first inning.

On a damp Monday night, Hampton beat the Cardinals, 7–0. The final out came on a fly to Timo Perez, a tiny outfielder from the Dominican Republic, who had played three seasons for the Hiroshima Carp in Japan before being released. In 2000, Perez had moved all the way up in the Mets' organization, joining the varsity in late summer, after which Valentine had boldly moved him ahead of three older outfielders.

Perez made several leaps while waiting for the ball to come down, and he gloved it, for the Mets' fourth pennant since their ghastly beginning under Casey Stengel in 1962.

The Mets had done their part. Now they had the delightful opportunity to sit back and wait to see what the Yankees would do. Would Mets' fans ever root for the Yankees to win anything? Or was the prospect of beating the Yankees in a Subway Series worth rooting for?

Wednesday, October 11, 2000

GAME 1

CARDINALS 0   METS 1

METS 6	GAME ONE – BUSCH STADIUM												CARDINALS 2
		1	2	3	4	5	6	7	8	9	H	E	
	Mets	2	0	0	0	1	0	0	0	0	3	8	3	
	Cardinals	0	0	0	0	0	0	0	0	2	9	0	

Scoring Summary: T1st: Piazza doubled to left, Perez scored, Alfonzo to third. Ventura hit sacrifice fly to left, Alfonzo scored. T5th: Alfonzo singled to left, Hampton scored. T9th: Zeile homered to left center. Payton homered to left, McEwing scored. B9th: Renteira safe at first on shortstop Abbott's throwing error, Lankford scored. Edmonds singled to right, Renteira to third. Renteira scored.

 We didn't have a prototypical leadoff hitter and we do in Timo. He gets on base, has some power and you've got one of the best clutch hitters in baseball hitting second. If Timo gets on, you know Fonzie's going to make something happen."

METS **BENNY AGBAYANI** ON THE DIFFERENCE THAT ROOKIE TIMO PEREZ (LEFT) HAS MADE TO THE LINE-UP

> 66 I liked the way we played, I just didn't like the final score. Hampton and the Mets were a little better."

CARDINALS MANAGER **TONY LA RUSSA**

> 66 Certainly Mike had his moments, but really what it is is mental toughness and making quality pitches when he had to, and he did that."

METS VETERAN PITCHER **AL LEITER**

> 66 There was only one inning where I retired the side in order, so there were always people on base and every pitch had some meaning behind it."

METS STARTING PITCHER **MIKE HAMPTON** (ABOVE)

METS RELIEVER JOHN FRANCO CONGRATULATES TODD ZEILE AFTER HIS NINTH-INNING SOLO HOMER

> 66 There had been some doubts cast over Mike because of a small sample of postseason play, and I think he erased those doubts."

METS MANAGER **BOBBY VALENTINE**

GAME 2

CARDINALS 0   METS 2

		1	2	3	4	5	6	7	8	9	H	E
METS 6	Mets	2	0	1	0	0	0	0	2	1	9	0
CARDINALS 5	Cardinals	0	1	0	0	2	0	0	2	0	10	3

GAME TWO – BUSCH STADIUM

Scoring Summary: T1st: Zeile hit sacrifice fly to center, Alfonzo scored. Agbayani doubled to left center, Piazza scored. B2nd: Marrero grounded out to second, Dunston scored. T3rd: Piazza homered to right. B5th: Renteria doubled to shallow left, Vina scored. Tatis doubled to left, Renteria scored. T8th: Alfonzo singled to right center, Perez scored, Alfonzo to second advancing on throw. Zeile singled to left, Alfonzo scored. B8th: Hernandez walks. Clark singled to right, Hernandez scored, Clark to second on wild pitch. Drew doubled to center, Clark scored. T9th: Payton singled to center, McEwing scored.

A DEJECTED RICK ANKIEL LEAVES THE MOUND AFTER HIS FIRST-INNING NIGHTMARE THAT LEFT THE CARDINALS TRAILING BY TWO

" Before anybody starts kicking Rick around, I think the blame is on me for putting him out there."

CARDINALS MANAGER **TONY LA RUSSA**

" It's unfortunate. I feel like I let this team down."

CARDINALS ROOKIE PITCHER **RICK ANKIEL** WHO HIT THE BACKSTOP WITH FIVE OF HIS FIRST 20 PITCHES.

JAY PAYTON (ABOVE) SLAPS A SINGLE UP THE MIDDLE IN THE NINTH TO GIVE THE METS A 6–5 LEAD. (INSET) JOE McEWING SCORES THE WINNING RUN ON PAYTON'S HIT

> ❝ We're not relying on one particular guy, so you've got everyone pulling for everyone else. But there's got to be more than that. A lot of guys in this room have great spirit and a lot of fight to them. We've played games like this so many times and had so much success, it gives us confidence that when our backs are against the wall, we're going to respond. ❞

FIRST BASEMAN **TODD ZEILE** ON THE SECRET OF THE METS SUCCESS

EDGARDO ALFONZO SNAPPED THE TIE WITH AN RBI SINGLE IN THE EIGHTH, PUTTING THE METS UP 4–3

Friday, October 13, 2000

GAME 3

CARDINALS 1   METS 2

CARDINALS 8

GAME THREE – WILLIAM A. SHEA STADIUM											
	1	2	3	4	5	6	7	8	9	H	E
Cardinals	2	0	2	1	3	0	0	0	0	14	0
Mets	1	0	0	1	0	0	0	0	0	7	1

METS 2

Scoring Summary: T1st: Edmonds doubled to left, Vina and Renteria scored. B1st: Piazza grounded into double play, Perez scored. T3rd: Lankford singled to right center, Renteria scored, Clark to third. Tatis hit sacrifice fly to right, Clark scored. T4th: Renteria singled to left center, Andy Benes scored. B4th: Payton grounded into double play second to first, Ventura scored. T5th: Hernandez singled to shallow left, Tatis scored, Drew to second. Vina reached on fielder's choice to second, Drew scored, Hernandez to third. Renteria grounded out to shortstop, Hernandez scored.

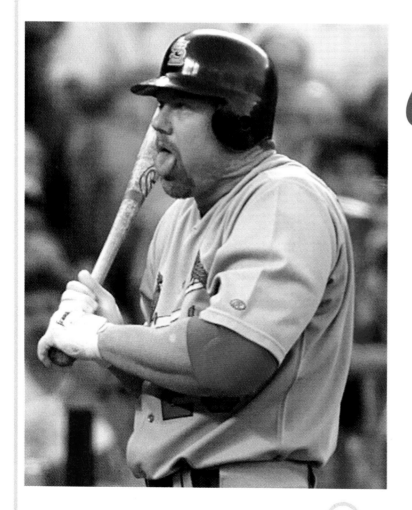

 We were just trying to add to the lead. There was a lot of game left. This was one of those situations that works best for Mark so I took a shot."

CARDINALS MANAGER **TONY LA RUSSA** ON HIS DECISION TO PINCH HIT MARK McGWIRE (LEFT) FOR RAY LANKFORD IN THE FOURTH. BIG MAC WAS RETIRED ON A FLY BALL TO LEFT FIELD

"He made really good pitches when he had to. We had him on the ropes a couple of times, but we couldn't put him away."

METS MANAGER **BOBBY VALENTINE** ON CARDINALS PITCHER ANDY BENES

"In St. Louis nobody is talking about the Subway Series. You come to New York and obviously that's what people here are pulling for, the home teams. We're not going to give in or give up. We come from the Midwest and that's not what people want there."

CARDINALS MANAGER **TONY LA RUSSA**

GAME 4

CARDINALS 1   METS 3

CARDINALS 6	GAME FOUR – WILLIAM A. SHEA STADIUM											METS 10

	1	2	3	4	5	6	7	8	9	H	E
Cardinals	2	0	0	1	3	0	0	0	0	11	2
Mets	4	3	0	1	0	2	0	0	x	9	0

Scoring Summary: T1st: Edmonds homerd to right center, Vina scored. B1st: Alfonzo doubled to right, Perez scored. Ventura doubled to deep right center, Alfonzo and Piazza scored. Agbayani doubled to deep center, Ventura scored. B2nd: Zeile doubled to left, Perez and Piazza scored, Ventura to third. Agbayani singled to center, Ventura scored. T4th: Clark homered to left center. B4th: Piazza homered to left. T5th: Davis doubled to left, Drew scored, Hernandez to third. Renteria hit sacrifice fly to right, Hernandez scored, Davis to third. Edmonds singled to right, Davis scored. B6th: Piazza safe at first on third baseman Tatis' fielding error, Bordick scored, Perez to third, Alfonzo to second. Ventura hit sacrifice fly to left, Perez scored.

> **"** He was firing, but everything was elevated. They didn't miss them. Usually that's what happens when they have too much rest."

CARDINALS MANAGER **TONY LA RUSSA** ON PITCHER DARRYL KILE WHO GAVE UP EIGHT HITS AND SEVEN RUNS IN HIS THREE-INNING OUTING

66 Those are three huge innings. We don't win the game without those three innings."

METS ARMANDO BENITEZ CLOSED IT OUT IN THE NINTH, GETTING JIM EDMONDS TO FLY OUT TO THE RIGHT TO END THE GAME

66 It would have been a lot more exciting if he had not made the play. He's the X-factor of X-factors. There were a few times he was standing there lurking in the wings. I'm glad we kept him on the bench."

METS MANAGER **BOBBY VALENTINE** ON TODD ZEILE'S PLAY TO END THE SIXTH INNING WITH MARK McGWIRE WAITING IN THE WINGS

MIKE PIAZZA ADDED TO THE METS LEAD WITH A SOLO HOMER IN THE FOURTH

66 I was going to wait until the tying run to put him up. When the tying run was up, he was coming up. But the tying run didn't come up."

CARDINALS MANAGER **TONY LA RUSSA** ON WHY MARK McGWIRE (LEFT) NEVER MADE IT TO THE PLATE

Monday, October 16, 2000

GAME 5

CARDINALS 1   METS 4

CARDINALS 0	GAME FIVE – WILLIAM A. SHEA STADIUM											METS 7
		1	2	3	4	5	6	7	8	9	H	E
	Cardinals	0	0	0	0	0	0	0	0	0	3	2
	Mets	3	0	0	3	0	0	1	0	x	10	0

Scoring Summary: B1st: Alfonzo singled to right, Perez scored. Ventura singled to right, Alfonzo scored, Piazza to third. Zeile grounded into fielder's choice to second, Piazza scored. B4th: Zeile doubled to deep right center, Perez, Piazza and Ventura scored. B7th: Bordick scored on Ankiel wild pitch.

"I got hit and ... my reactions got the best of me. I don't know if there was any intent there. I don't think there was"

METS **JAY PAYTON** (LEFT) WHO WAS HIT ON THE HELMET BY DAVE VERES IN THE EIGHTH, WAS CUT AND CHARGED THE MOUND PROMPTING THE EMPTYING OF BOTH DUGOUTS AND BULLPENS

"" We have some experience; we went through it a year ago. The other big difference is our pitching is just that tick better than it was a year ago. We're stronger at the front of our rotation, and a little deeper in the bullpen."

METS GENERAL MANAGER **STEVE PHILLIPS** ON THE DIFFERENCE A YEAR MAKES

"" It's what you play for and what you put all the hard work in for. We're happy to go right now. It would be nice to stay at home, though."

METS THIRD BASEMAN **ROBIN VENTURA**
(BELOW) ON REACHING THE WORLD SERIES

"" We had enough weapons to win. The Mets just played better."

CARDINALS MANAGER **TONY LA RUSSA**

"We're prepared for an absolutely incredible Series."

NEW YORK MAYOR RUDOLPH W. GIULIANI

> "The team needed a big game. We're close. We're four games away from fulfilling that fantasy."

METS PITCHER **MIKE HAMPTON**

The World Series

AMERICAN
LEAGUE

YANKEES

VS

NATIONAL
LEAGUE

METS

THE CITY WAS
IN A HUBBUB, WITH
ENTREPRENEURS
KNOCKING OUT
T-SHIRTS AND
TELEVISION STATIONS
AND NEWSPAPERS
UNABLE TO GET
ENOUGH OF IT.
FINALLY, THE SUBWAY
SERIES BEGAN.

	MF		GAME ONE – YANKEE STADIUM													

GAME ONE – YANKEE STADIUM													
	1	2	3	4	5	6	7	8	9	10	11	12	H	E
Mets	0	0	0	0	0	0	3	0	0	0	0	0	10	0
Yankees	0	0	0	0	0	2	0	0	1	0	0	1	12	0

METS 3   **YANKEES 4**

Scoring Summary: B6th: Justice doubled to deep left center, Knoblauch and Jeter scored. T7th: Trammell singled to left, Agbayani and Payton scored, Pratt to second. Alfonzo reached on an infield single, Pratt scored. B9th: Knoblauch hit sacrifice fly to left, O'Neill scored. B12th: Vizcaino singled to left, Martinez scored.

FOUR OUT OF SEVEN DOESN'T LEAVE MUCH ROOM FOR ERROR. THE FIRST GAME WAS THE LONGEST IN WORLD SERIES HISTORY, LONG ENOUGH FOR MOOD SWINGS, LONG ENOUGH FOR THE METS TO MEANDER THEIR WAY INTO TROUBLE, LONG ENOUGH FOR THE YANKEES TO ESTABLISH THEIR POISE, QUITE LONG ENOUGH FOR THE RIVAL BULLPENS TO SET OPPOSITE TONES.

World Series – Game One

The feel of the World Series had changed almost totally in the 44 years since both teams hailed from New York. In those days, the games were played in the early afternoon, in hazy sunshine mostly, but now, because of the demands of television, the games began at 8pm or later, and seemed to last forever, as batters fiddled with their equipment and pitchers fidgeted on the mound.

As a result, the future fan base in New York, young children, would never see the endings of five taut games, particularly the opening game, which became the longest in the history of the World Series: 4 hours and 51 minutes.

The Mets blew a major chance in the sixth when rookie Timo Perez did not run hard on a long drive by Todd Zeile that bounced off the very top of the leftfield fence. Finally in gear, Perez was thrown out at the plate on a marvelous relay from Justice to Jeter to Jorge Posada. Several Mets' veterans would chide Perez about not hustling, but in a short series like this, serious damage was already done.

The Mets had a 3–2 lead on a two-run pinch single by Bubba Trammell going into the ninth. However, Armando Benitez, the ace reliever, was worn down by Paul O'Neill, who fouled off four straight

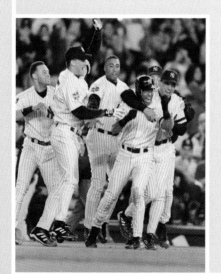

pitches and on the tenth pitch walked. This set up a game-tying sacrifice fly by Knoblauch, who was the designated hitter because Torre decided not to use his wobbly arm at second base. In the 12th, the Yankees won on a single by Jose Vizcaino, who had started in place of Knoblauch.

The Yankees' bullpen worked, the Mets' did not — an extremely telltale sign.

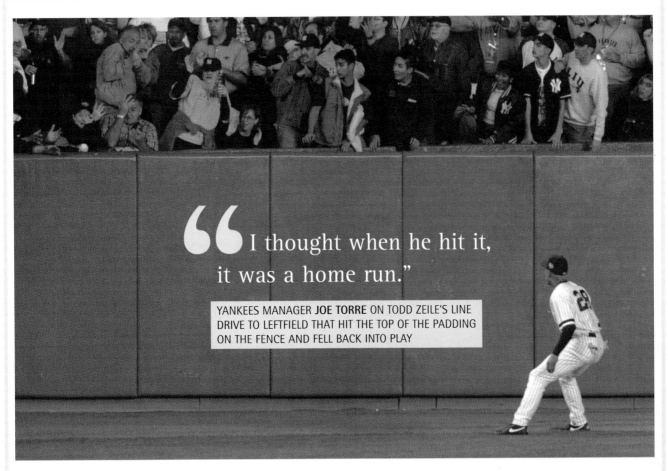

"I thought when he hit it, it was a home run."

"I saw him out of the corner of my eye. And I saw he hadn't reached third yet. So I thought, 'If I get rid of this as fast as I can, I might have a shot at him.' In that situation, as fast as he is, I knew I didn't have time to plant my feet. So I just grabbed it and threw it."

YANKEES **DEREK JETER** ON THE IMPROBABLE THROW HE MADE FROM SHORT LEFTFIELD TO NAIL PEREZ AT THE PLATE

TIMO PEREZ'S ERROR ON THE BASE PATHS IN THE SIXTH INNNING COST THE METS DEARLY

THE METS AL LEITER (BELOW) LEAVES THE FIELD AFTER SURRENDERING A TWO-RUN DOUBLE TO DAVID JUSTICE (ABOVE) THAT PUT THE YANKEES UP 2–0

" It was probably the most exciting one. And, obviously, the longest one. But I'd also have to say it was the most gratifying one."

YANKEES **DEREK JETER** ON GAME 1

BUBBA TRAMMELL CONNECTS FOR A TWO-RUN SINGLE IN THE SEVENTH THAT TIED IT UP AT 2–2

" We've been through a whole bunch of nerve-racking games. These guys have the heart of a lion."

YANKEES OWNER **GEORGE STEINBRENNER**

" It was heart-stopping at times. It was kind of ugly at times. But it was a great Game One. If they're all like this, buckle your seat belts. This should be some kind of Series. If that's Game One, look out."

YANKEES **DAVID CONE**

" I thought it was a heck of a game. Two teams that battled their way to get here battled their way tonight."

METS MANAGER **BOBBY VALENTINE**

" We came in with very little World Series experience and got a lot of it in one night."

METS MANAGER **BOBBY VALENTINE**

" I'd like to believe we find a way to win."

YANKEES MANAGER **JOE TORRE**

"I was thinking I would be going to the World Series, but I didn't think I'd be the hero in the first game."

YANKEES **JOSE VIZCAINO**, ONE OF EIGHT YANKEES ACQUIRED IN MIDSEASON NOW ON THEIR POSTSEASON ROSTER. AN EX-MET, HE ARRIVED FROM THE LOS ANGELES DODGERS IN JUNE

THE YANKEES JOSE VIZCAINO CELEBRATES HIS GAME-WINNING SINGLE IN THE BOTTOM OF THE 12TH TO GIVE HIS TEAM A 1–0 SERIES LEAD. (RIGHT) CELEBRATION TIME FOR THE YANKEES

"I'm just gonna go home now and think about all the at-bats and picture myself doing it again – because I'm never going to forget this day."

YANKEES **JOSE VIZCAINO**

"This feeling is going to last a long time. I'm never gonna forget this."

YANKEES **JOSE VIZCAINO**

"I was listening to the crowd. They were all screaming – because they wanted the game to be over."

YANKEES **JOSE VIZCAINO**

Sunday, October 22, 2000

METS 0   2   YANKEES 2

Scoring Summary: B1st: Martinez singled to left, Justice scored, Williams to second. Posada singled to center, Williams scored. B2nd: Brosius homered to left. B5th: O'Neill singled to right, Martinez scored. B7th: Brosius hit sacrifice fly, Posada scored. B8th: Martinez singled to shallow left center, Jeter scored. T9th: Piazza homered to left, Alfonzo scored. Payton homered to right, Agbayani and Harris scored.

THERE WAS A LOT OF HISTORY TO THIS GAME, INVOLVING MIKE PIAZZA AND ROGER CLEMENS. IN JULY, DURING AN INTERLEAGUE GAME, CLEMENS HAD THROWN INSIDE TO PIAZZA, WHO WAS 7–12 AGAINST HIM WITH THREE HOMERS. THE BALL HIT PIAZZA IN THE HELMET, SENDING HIM OUT OF THE GAME WITH A CONCUSSION. THE NEXT CONFRONTATION WOULD TURN OUT TO BE MORE BIZARRE THAN ANYBODY COULD HAVE ANTICIPATED.

World Series – Game Two

With two outs in the first inning, Clemens was visibly tense, muttering and stomping around the mound. Piazza swung and his bat broke, a normal occurrence, sending one large chunk sailing toward the mound.

Clemens instinctively picked up the jagged piece of bat, but then, inexplicably, slung it dangerously close to Piazza who was jogging toward first base, not knowing the ball had gone foul. When the bat missed Piazza by a foot or two, he turned toward the mound, asking "What's your problem?"

Both benches emptied but no punches were thrown. When things quieted down, Clemens pitched nearly as masterfully as he had in his previous start in Seattle, giving up only two hits and striking out nine in eight innings. In the ninth, Piazza hit a two-run homer off Jeff Nelson, and Jay Payton hit a three-run homer off a weary Rivera, but the Mets fell short.

Later, Clemens explained his actions: "I was taking a bat and throwing it to our on-deck circle. I wish it would have been somebody completely different – then it wouldn't have meant anything. I don't want to revisit it."

Piazza would say: "He seemed extremely apologetic and unsure and confused and unstable."

Everybody wondered if there would be a rematch in a sixth game at Yankee Stadium.

66 Let's try to analyze it: Why would he throw it at him? So he could get thrown out of the game in the second game of the World Series? Does that make any sense to anybody? Somebody answer me?"

66 It was just so bizarre. When he threw the bat, I basically walked out and kept asking him what his problem was. He really had no response. I was trying to figure out whether it was intentional or not. I was going to ask him. If it was, then obviously he really had no response. I was more shocked and confused than anything."

66 There was no intent. I was fired up and emotional and flung the bat toward the on-deck circle where the batboy was. I had no idea that Mike was running ... I guess it came close to him. I came back into the dugout and I said, 'I've got to get control of my emotions and calm down.'"

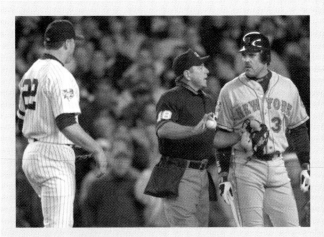

> **"** I was looking at the ball, the ball went foul and I'm running toward first base and, all of a sudden ... basically I don't know what happened.
>
> "I didn't say anything to Piazza. I just said 'Let's play ball.'"

YANKEES CATCHER **JORGE POSADA**

❝ I certainly wasn't calling for his suspension from the Series and I don't think any of our players are looking for him to be suspended. Our preference is that if we have a chance to win the World Series, we'd like to do it with both teams at full strength."

METS GENERAL MANAGER **STEVE PHILLIPS**

❝ This is the World Series. If you think that you go out there and you are robots and you throw the ball, you catch the ball, and that's what you do ... you have to be emotional and you have to be passionate. Am I saying that he should have picked up the bat and thrown it? No. I think it was an emotional thing. I think Roger will tell you that he was very surprised when he looked up, that Piazza was where he was."

YANKEES MANAGER **JOE TORRE**

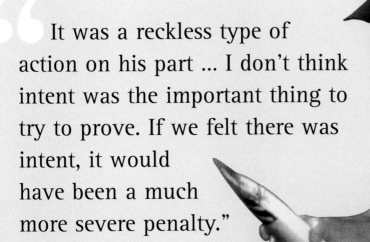

" It was a reckless type of action on his part ... I don't think intent was the important thing to try to prove. If we felt there was intent, it would have been a much more severe penalty."

FRANK ROBINSON, BASEBALL'S VICE PRESIDENT OF OPERATIONS

" I want to stay focused on the task at hand, helping my team win the World Series, so I do not intend to consider the question of an appeal or respond to questions about the fine or the incident itself until the Series is over."

A STATEMENT FROM **ROGER CLEMENS** AFTER NEWS OF HIS $50,000 FINE

" With all the stuff I had to listen to leading up to the game, I had to get control of my emotions. I was fired up."

YANKEES **ROGER CLEMENS**

"We can stand here and harp all night about what he did. But the bottom line is, he beat us. And the only way for us to get back at him was to beat him. And we didn't do it."

METS MANAGER **BOBBY VALENTINE**

"He was able to use our aggressiveness against us."

METS **TODD ZEILE**

"Maybe if you are down 0-2, maybe you should choose to make more of that then you possibly should. Remember when we were down 2-0 to Atlanta? We just went and played the game. That's all."

YANKEES OWNER **GEORGE STEINBRENNER**

(FAR RIGHT) THE METS MIKE PIAZZA AND EDGARDO ALFONZO CELEBRATE AFTER PIAZZA'S TWO-RUN DINGER IN THE NINTH

THIRD BASEMAN SCOTT BROSIUS PUTS THE YANKEES AHEAD WITH HIS SOLO BLAST IN THE SECOND INNING

DEREK JETER SCORES AN INSURANCE RUN IN THE EIGHTH TO GIVE THE YANKEES A SEEMINGLY UNASSAILABLE LEAD

Tuesday, October 24, 2000

YANKEES 2	GAME THREE – WILLIAM A. SHEA STADIUM													METS 4
		1	2	3	4	5	6	7	8	9	H	E	
	Yankees	0	0	1	1	0	0	0	0	0	8	0	
	Mets	0	1	0	0	0	1	0	2	x	9	0	

Scoring Summary: B2nd: Ventura homered to right. T3rd: Justice doubled to shallow right, Jeter scored. T4th: O'Neill tripled to right center, Martinez scored. B6th: Zeile doubled to left, Piazza scored. B8th: Agbayani doubled to left center, Zeile scored. Trammell hit sacrifice fly to center, McEwing scored.

THE SERIES MOVED OVER TO QUEENS ON THE NO. 7 TRAIN, AND BASEBALL OFFICIALS ANNOUNCED THAT, AFTER AN INVESTIGATION BY FRANK ROBINSON, ROGER CLEMENS HAD BEEN FINED $50,000 FOR HIS FOOLISH BEHAVIOR. THE YANKEES STARTER ORLANDO HERNANDEZ WAS RUMORED TO BE NOT FEELING WELL. FOR THE METS, BACK AT SHEA AND TWO DOWN, ANY LIFELINE WOULD BE APPRECIATED.

World Series – Game Three

Justice and O'Neill drove in early runs for the Yankees against Rick Reed, a journeyman right-hander. "El Duque" struck out the side in the first two innings, giving up a solo homer to Robin Ventura. In the sixth inning, Piazza doubled and Zeile tied the score with a double.

Hernandez, who had impressed Torre with his poise after his mysterious escape from Cuba by sea, was able to persuade the manager to go back to the mound for the eighth inning of the 2–2 tie. He had earned this right with pressure performances when the Yankees were in trouble in other championship games.

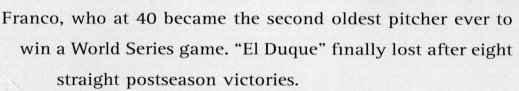

This time, however, Zeile singled, Benny Agbayani doubled for a run and Payton hit a single up the middle. Mike Stanton replaced "El Duque" and gave up a sacrifice fly to Bubba Trammell. Then Benitez saved the victory for John Franco, who at 40 became the second oldest pitcher ever to win a World Series game. "El Duque" finally lost after eight straight postseason victories.

Even though the Mets won, they were stunned to hear the large contingent of Yankee fans, who had apparently paid steep scalping prices. The operative theory was that the Yankees, by winning three recent World Series, had developed a huge following of fans, who would stop at nothing to get their hands on tickets. The Mets were too professional to let it affect their play, but they noticed.

ROBIN VENTURA GOES DEEP TO GIVE THE METS AN EARLY LEAD

" Our fans have been waiting 14 years for this. They're very loud and we just love being in this ballpark and the noise."

METS WINNING PITCHER **JOHN FRANCO**

" A lot of people don't like to play here. The field ... there's airplanes going overhead – we feel comfortable here. It's loud."

METS **TODD ZEILE** ON THE NUANCES OF SHEA

PAUL O'NEILL'S TRIPLE IN THE FOURTH INNING SCORES TINO MARTINEZ, AS THE YANKS TAKE A 2–1 LEAD

"It was typical El Duque. He's up on that high wire all the time. You don't think he's going to be able to get down from there. He has good stuff, but his determination is really tough. He's really tough when it comes to big games."

YANKEES MANAGER **JOE TORRE**

"All we ever heard was how he won all those games and had never lost. There's the first time for everyone."

METS **BENNY AGBAYANI** ON THE HYPE SURROUNDING ORLANDO "EL DUQUE" HERNANDEZ

"Twelve strikeouts. It's not important. What's important is that I could not get Agbayani out. That's more important than 12 strikeouts."

YANKEES PITCHER **ORLANDO HERNANDEZ** ON AGBAYANI'S GAME-WINNING DOUBLE IN THE EIGHTH

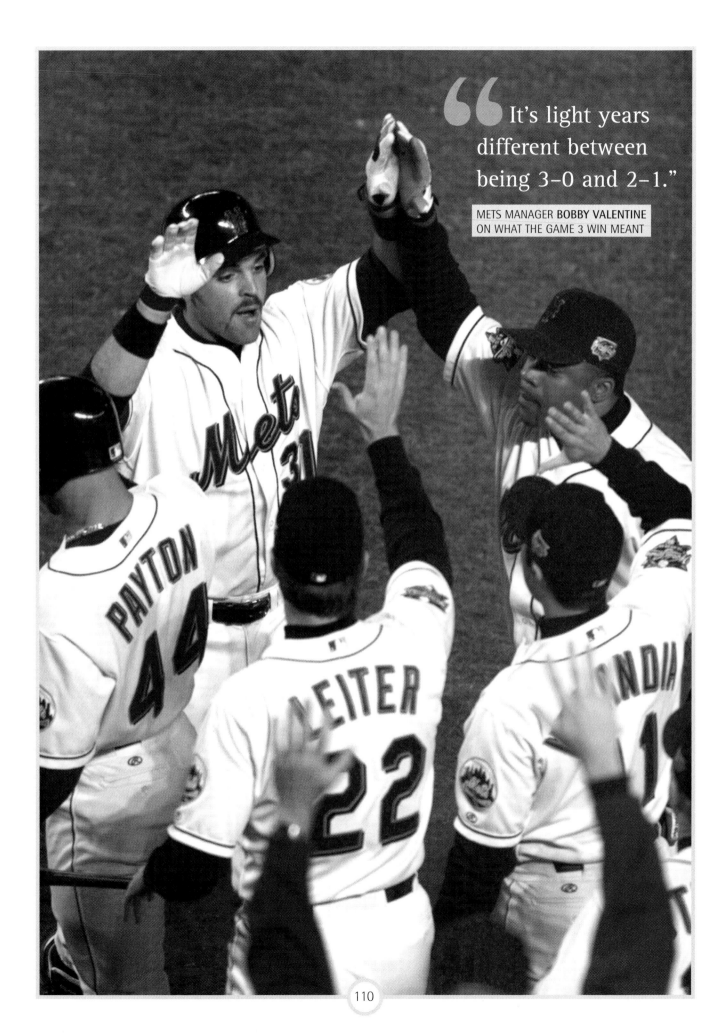

" It's light years different between being 3–0 and 2–1."

METS MANAGER **BOBBY VALENTINE**
ON WHAT THE GAME 3 WIN MEANT

THE METS CELEBRATE (ABOVE), WHILE THE YANKEES (BELOW) TRY TO THINK ABOUT TOMORROW

"I think we have been down this road so many times, not necessarily in the World Series, but we've been here. We've been pretty good responding to losses and hopefully we'll do it again tomorrow."

YANKEES MANAGER JOE TORRE

Wednesday, October 25, 2000

4

METS 1   YANKEES 3

YANKEES 3	GAME FOUR – WILLIAM A. SHEA STADIUM											METS 2
		1	2	3	4	5	6	7	8	9	H	E
	Yankees	1	1	1	0	0	0	0	0	0	8	0
	Mets	0	0	2	0	0	0	0	0	0	6	1

Scoring Summary: T1st: Jeter homered to left. T2nd: Brosius hit sacrifice fly to center, O'Neill scored. T3rd: Sojo grounded out to second, Jeter scored. B3rd: Piazza homered to left, Perez scored.

THE METS EUPHORIA DID NOT LAST LONG. JUST BEFORE THE GAME, THE YANKEES DEREK JETER SPOTTED HIS PAL, ALEX RODRIGUEZ, THE MARINERS SOON-TO-BE FREE AGENT WHO WAS IN TOWN FOR BUSINESS. THE TWO FRIENDS CHATTED FOR A FEW MINUTES, AND THEN RODRIGUEZ TURNED TO HIS AGENT AND SAID, "WATCH, HE'LL SWING AT THE FIRST PITCH."

World Series – Game Four

Jeter promptly led off the game with a home run on the first pitch from Bobby J. Jones.

In the second, O'Neill tripled and scored on a fly. And in the third, Jeter tripled and scored on a grounder by the venerable Luis Sojo, playing second base.

The Mets knew this was the one game they needed to win, against Denny Neagle, a left-hander who was in Torre's doghouse for his hesitant ways. The Mets scored twice in the third on a two-run homer by Piazza.

With two outs in the fifth, and Piazza coming up, Torre made one of his characteristically fearless moves, removing Neagle for David Cone, the 37-year-old righty who had pitched a perfect game in 1999, but had just concluded a dreadful and injury-marked season and also had rarely worked in relief. Cone induced Piazza to pop to second, and then the bullpen combo of Jeff Nelson, Mike Stanton and Rivera shut down the Mets for the last four innings.

The Mets trudged back to their clubhouse, knowing they had just blown a major opportunity.

Would there ever be a Subway Series matching Jeter of the Yanks with Rodriguez of the Mets? Rodriguez played it coy on that one. This Series belonged to his pal.

DAVID JUSTICE GIVES DEREK JETER CONGRATULATIONS AFTER HIS FIRST-INNING BLAST OPENED GAME 4 WITH A BANG

" Everyone seems to want to ask me if I change my approach. But Mr Torre tells me to have the same approach. When you play in these types of games when runs can be hard to come by, you want to score early. I got a good pitch to hit and I hit it well and fortunately it carried out."

YANKEES **DEREK JETER** WHO SWUNG ON THE FIRST PITCH OF THE BALLGAME FOR A HOMER BECOMING THE FIRST YANKEE BATTER TO DO SO SINCE GENE WOODLING IN GAME 5 OF THE 1953 SERIES

" I'd been watching films of the way Jeter had approached the at-bats against our other pitchers, and he seemed to work deep in the count a lot. He seemed very patient. I hadn't seen anything that told me he'd be swinging right away."

METS PITCHER **BOBBY J. JONES** WHO SERVED UP DEREK JETER'S FIRST-PITCH DINGER

"When Derek steps into the box, that's what makes him so dangerous. You definitely don't want to get him on base via the walk because he has the great hitters behind him.

But he's so aggressive ... you have to be careful.

I knew he would swing at the first pitch."

THE MARINERS **ALEX RODRIGUEZ** ON HIS CLOSE FRIEND'S ATTITUDE AT THE PLATE

"I've been known to swing at the first pitch. When you play games like this, you want to score early. I got a good pitch to hit, and I hit it well ... We're playing at Shea Stadium, and even though there are a few Yankee fans here, you want to take the crowd out of the game."

YANKEES DEREK JETER

> "As great as they are during the season, they take it to another level this time of year. We have a long road ahead of us now."
>
> METS **BENNY AGBAYANI** ON THE YANKEES POSTSEASON DOMINANCE

> "Putting a run on the board was the difference in the game."
>
> METS MANAGER **BOBBY VALENTINE**

> "We played a great game in every game. Every single one has been close. And we're still down. We're going to find a way to win three straight. It won't be easy, but we're going to do it."
>
> METS MANAGER **BOBBY VALENTINE**

MIKE PIAZZA'S TWO-RUN HOMER BROUGHT THE METS TO WITHIN ONE RUN, BUT THE YANKEES BULLPEN PROVED TOO STRONG

❝ He makes things happen. The kid has only been around five years, but he's got all the qualities of someone who takes charge and leads by example as opposed to telling everybody that he's the leader of the club."

YANKEES MANAGER **JOE TORRE** ON DEREK JETER, WHOSE WORLD SERIES HIT STREAK NOW STANDS AT 13 GAMES

❝ We're one win from where we want to be."

YANKEES MANAGER **JOE TORRE**

MARIANO RIVERA PITCHED TWO SHUTOUT INNINGS AS THE YANKEES CLOSED IT OUT TO LEAD THE SERIES 3–1

Thursday, October 26, 2000

METS
1

5

YANKEES
4

YANKEES 4	GAME FIVE – WILLIAM A. SHEA STADIUM											METS 2

	1	2	3	4	5	6	7	8	9	H	E
Yankees	0	1	0	0	0	1	0	0	2	7	1
Mets	0	2	0	0	0	0	0	0	0	8	1

Scoring Summary: T2nd: Williams homered to left. B2nd: Leiter safe at first on pitcher Pettitte's fielding error, Trammell scored, Payton to third. Agbayani reached on an infield single, Payton scored. T6th: Jeter homered to left. T9th: Sojo singled to shallow center, Posada scored. Brosius scored after Payton's throw to home bounced off Posada into Yankees dugout.

LONG AFTER MIDNIGHT, IN THE PARKING

LOTS OUTSIDE SHEA STADIUM, THE CRY OF

"LET'S GO, YAN-KEES!" COULD BE HEARD.

IN THE BACKGROUND, YOU COULD HEAR THE

NO. 7 TRAIN, RUMBLING NORMALLY, AS IF

OBLIVIOUS TO THE MIXTURE OF JOY AND PAIN

AFFLICTING VARIOUS NEW YORKERS AT THE

END OF THIS SUBWAY SERIES.

World Series – Game Five

With no margin for error, the Mets sent out Al Leiter against dependable Andy Pettitte.

Bernie Williams cracked a home run to lead off the second, his first hit in the Series. The Mets went ahead, 2-1, in the second on a walk, a single, an error by Pettitte and a single by Agbayani.

In the sixth, Jeter tied the score with a home run. The two lefties staged a duel through seven innings, and Stanton stopped the Mets in the eighth. Leiter was still in the game in the ninth, striking out the first two hitters. He walked Posada. Then Scott Brosius smacked a single to left.

On Leiter's 142nd pitch, Sojo slapped a single up the middle. Jay Payton charged the ball and heaved it homeward. The ball ticked the sliding Posada and ricocheted into the Mets' dugout, with Brosius scoring automatically.

The Yankees traded high fives in their dugout. Rivera came in for the ninth and got two around Agbayani walking and taking second. Then it was Rivera against Piazza for the 27th out. Piazza struck a long fly to center field, but Bernie Williams was there, and the Yankees were now the first team since the 1972–74 Oakland Athletics to win three straight World Series.

The Yankees fell in a pile on the mound and soon celebrated with champagne in the visiting clubhouse. Steinbrenner and Torre seemed exhausted from the difficult season, declining to say whether he would come back for another try. Jeter, the latest in a long line of superstars, was named the Most Valuable Player of the Series.

The Mets were disconsolate but knew they had been close in every game against a team they now respected more than ever.

" The Mets are – in my opinion – the best team we've played in my years here."

" The Mets gave us everything we could want. It was great for the city of New York. I hope we don't have to go through this again for another 44 years."

" This was super satisfying. It's never easy, but we had a lot of trouble putting things together this year."

BERNIE WILLIAMS BROKE OUT OF HIS SLUMP WITH A HOMER IN THE SECOND INNING OFF THE METS AL LEITER

DEREK JETER'S WORLD SERIES HIT STREAK CONTINUED WITH HIS SOLO BLAST IN THE SIXTH INNING

(ABOVE) JORGE POSADA'S NINE-PITCH AT-BAT PROVED CRUCIAL AS HIS WALK TURNED INTO THE WINNING RUN IN THE NINTH. THE YANKEES SCORED AGAIN, AS BROSIUS JOINED POSADA ON JAY PAYTON'S THROWING ERROR.
(RIGHT) JORGE POSADA (20) AND SCOTT BROSIUS (18) RECEIVE SOME LOVE AFTER SCORING ON LUIS SOJO'S NINTH-INNING SINGLE

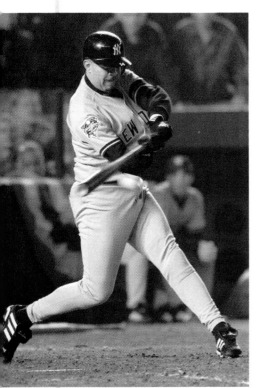

" I'd be lying if I said this one wasn't more gratifying. I mean, we struggled this year. We had tough times."

SERIES MVP **DEREK JETER**. THE YANKEES 87 REGULAR SEASON WINS WERE THE FEWEST AMONG ALL POSTSEASON TEAMS IN 2000

" It's the happiest day of my life. I don't know how to explain it. Today they gave me a chance to come through. I did and it was unbelievable."

YANKEES **LUIS SOJO** (LEFT) WHO DROVE IN THE WINNING RUN WITH A BORROWED BAT

"I couldn't ask anything more of a group of guys. I couldn't ask for a better effort, for better preparation, for better camaraderie. They're the National League champs. I think that they were champs in this World Series, and I'm extremely proud of them."

METS MANAGER **BOBBY VALENTINE**

"There's nobody in here that should be ashamed of the season we had. It was just that the Yankees were a little bit better."

METS PITCHER **JOHN FRANCO**

"We lost to a very good team. We played them as tough as we could possibly play them. We have a strong nucleus and there's no reason we can't be back again next year and learn from this and hopefully win."

METS GENERAL MANAGER **STEVE PHILLIPS**

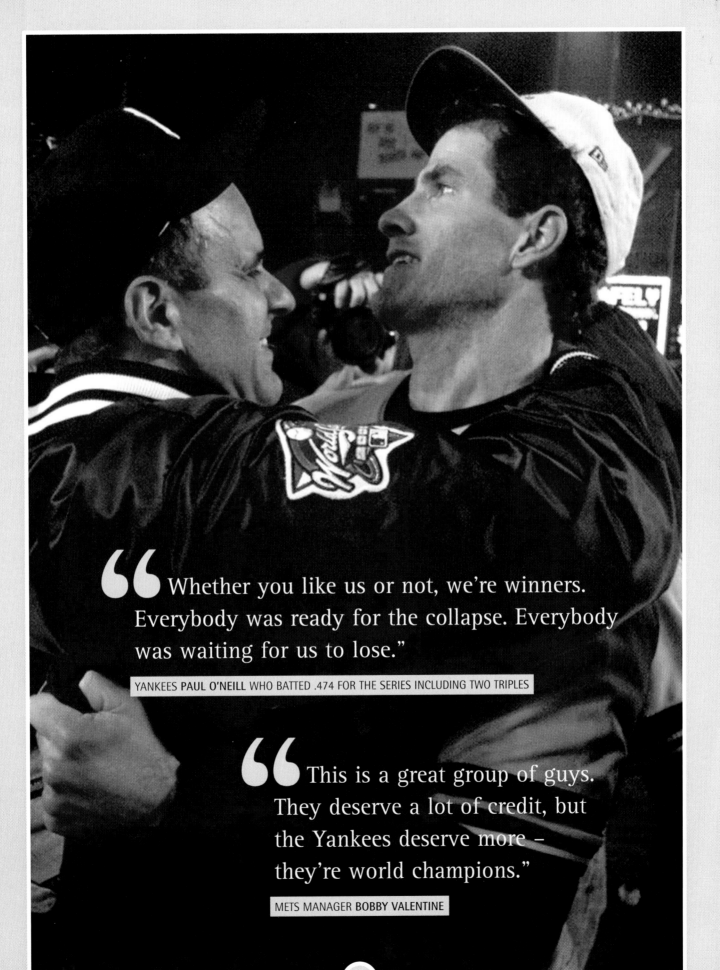

"Whether you like us or not, we're winners. Everybody was ready for the collapse. Everybody was waiting for us to lose."

YANKEES **PAUL O'NEILL** WHO BATTED .474 FOR THE SERIES INCLUDING TWO TRIPLES

"This is a great group of guys. They deserve a lot of credit, but the Yankees deserve more – they're world champions."

METS MANAGER **BOBBY VALENTINE**

Acknowledgments

In appreciation for all their efforts, the publishers would like to thank the following:
DAVID ELLIS (Yankees) for his greater knowledge and attention to detail, THOM & LIAM DUFFY (Mets) for the late night updates and general enthusiasm, NIGEL DAVIS, JOHNNY PAU and LUKE FRIEND for all their hard work into the late hours, and FIONA MARSH, JOSHUA & HANNAH PORTER for being patient.

Picture Credits

The publishers would like to thank the following sources for their kind permission to reproduce the pictures in this book:

Allsport USA 91, 106 cr, 108, 109, 110/Archives Photos 15, Al Bello 2-3, 68, 81, 88bl, 94, 106bl, Jonathan Daniel 71bl, 73, Tom Hauck 21tr, 21bl, 24br, 37, 39tr, 62, 97, Harry How 29tl, 29bl, 34cr, 34bl, 35bl, 68cr, Jed Jacobsohn 19, 22, 30, 31,33cr, 51, 86, 88, 97, 98, 99, 111, M David Leeds 24, 25,29bl, 55bl, 56, 78cr,79tr, Ezra Shaw 34tl, 35tr, 42, 42-3, 44, 49, 69br, 69tr, 69cl, 84, 93, 96tr, 96bl, 97c, 98bl, 104, 106, 107

Corbis/UPI 8-9, 11, 13bl, 14tl

AP Photo /Lynsey Addario 6, Mary Butkus 73t, James A. Finley 72, 73, Ron Frehm 68bl ,75, 79bl, 81br, 89t, 100, 101, 120, 124 t, 125, Bob Galbraith 17, 18tl, 20, 23, 58, 59br, 61,Tom Gannam 71, Chris Gardner 33 bl, Cheryl Hatch 59tl, 60, Harry How 46t, Charlie Krupa 51bl, 66, 76-7, 79cr, 84r, 112, 114bl, 118br, 122tr, 124bl, 126bl, 127 ,Bill Kostroun 16, 26-7, 40, 55t, 80, 90tl, 107t, 116-7, 122cl, Mark Lennihan 1, 3, 28, 46br, 47, 50tr, 57, 67, 92, 94, 102br, 111, 118, Ben Margot 18, 32, 33t, 37, Douglas C. Pizac 65, 65br, Suzanne Plunkett 7, 53, 54, Ed Reinke 70, Eric Risberg 38, 39, Amy Sancetta 89br, 90tr,90bl, 102tr, 103, 114, 115, 123 br, 123 tr, 126 t, 128, Andre Savulich, Pool 119, Matt York 36, 41, Ted S. Warren 48, 63, 64, Jeff Zelevansky 29, 44 bl, 45, 52, 74, 78, 82-3

Transcendental Graphics 10tl, 10b, 12, 13tr, 14br

Every effort has been made to acknowledge correctly and contact the source and/copyright holder of each picture, and Carlton Books Limited apologises for any unintentional errors or omissions which will be corrected in future editions of this book.

Special thanks to Jane Gowman at AP, Helen Dobson at Corbis UK and Paul Ashman at Allsport UK Ltd.